PEDAGOGY
OF THE CITY

PAULO FREIRE

PEDAGOGY OF THE CITY

Translated by Donaldo Macedo

CONTINUUM • NEW YORK

1993

The Continuum Publishing Company
370 Lexington Avenue
New York, NY 10017

Printed in the United States of America

Library of Congress Cataloging-in-Publication Data

Freire, Paulo, 1921–
    [Educação na cidate. English]
    Pedagogy of the city / Paulo Freire.
        p.   cm.
    Translation of: A educação na cidate.
    ISBN 0-8264-0612-2 (hardcover)
    1. Education—Brazil—São Paulo.   2. Popular education—Brazil–
–São Paulo.   I. Title.
LA559.S29F7413   1993
370'.981'61—dc20   92-29488
                                                          CIP

Contents

Epilogue

Postscript

Preliminary Considerations

The book that I have now given to the attention of potential readers will be published simultaneously here and in France. It is an unpretentious book, which, nonetheless, pleases me. If this were not the case, I would not publish it. The book is comprised of interviews that took place between the first months after I took the leadership of the Municipal Bureau of Education of São Paulo and the beginnings of the second year of our administration up to, and including, my farewell comments to others in the Bureau upon my retirement.

Some themes that were dealt with in the interviews did not reach the depth of development that we had anticipated. The majority of issues that we discuss, however, were realized in practice.

This book is, in reality, an introductory discussion of what we collectively dreamed of doing, what we did, and what continues to be done in the Municipal Bureau of Education of São Paulo. Other books and articles will come. They will emerge as an exercise of duty, a duty that makes us accountable to the city and to the nation to report and analyze not only what we have achieved, but also what we were not able to accomplish.

Paulo Freire
São Paulo, Spring, 1991

Preface

by Harold Raynolds, Jr.
Former Commissioner of Education, Massachusetts

Paulo Freire demonstrates in these dialogues that he is a philosopher-theoretician and an effective practitioner. In his role as Secretary of Education for the City of São Paulo he put his theories into practice and confronted again the awful struggle to get the resources to make education work for all children.

His observation confirms the central thesis that public education must play a decisive role in the continuing reformation of a democratic society in which all of us can have the freedom and opportunity to create knowledge from our own experience.

Poor and inadequate schools serve poor and disadvantaged children badly. Children of affluence can survive inadequate schools because of their advantages. Poor children are increasing in number and proportion in the United States and all over the world. The struggle against illiteracy is still a losing cause.

9

The crisis in schooling is urgent and becoming greater every day. The widening gulf between the haves and the have-nots compels us to seek a transformation of society in which education must play a role. For education to play that role each student must become "unquietly critical, challenged to understand that the world which is being presented as given is, in fact, a world being made, and for this very reason it can be changed, transformed, and reinvented." Knowledge, like human society, is not static and unchanging. All the classics have not been written. Basic science is still largely unrevealed. Wisdom is not finite.

What Paulo Freire experienced in São Paulo is not unique. For more than ten years the United States has reduced its proportionate share of support for public education, turned away from full funding of early childhood education and literacy campaigns. But the great assault has come on the public schools themselves. It is an orchestrated effort by education conservatives to retain and foster the growth of an elitist system of schooling insulated from and impervious to students from increasingly varied economic, social, and ethnic backgrounds.

Increased testing, which is fundamentally useless, has stigmatized students and schools for "failing" to meet the prescribed, accepted, or "received" truth based on the concept of a static and finite body of knowledge.

The result is a widening gulf, reduced resources, and such clever income transfer mechanisms as "choice" and voucher plans to take funding from the public treasury and give the dollars (vouchers) to advantaged parents. Thus, competition to the contrary, the public schools are further weakened, tested again, and punished in a round of punitive efforts that miss the mark of a public school in which students make knowledge of their own experience and learn to take an active role in the continuing transformation of society.

Public schools in São Paulo and Boston also need protection from "Education Presidents" and "Education Governors" who have benefited from selected expensive schools, colleges, and universities designed to produce a cultivated elite to manage and govern an essentially static society. Instead of working to create schools for all that provide the benefits of such schooling, these elected officials fail to recognize what Paulo Freire describes as the transformation of society based on the actual conditions in the population and the society. Failure to respond in an evolutionary way by providing opportunities for all children rich and poor is shortsighted and dangerous.

Paulo Freire does more in these dialogues. In addition to providing the basic reason for the construction of dynamic and responsive schools, he offers an action plan for the transformation of schooling. All of these are parts of that plan:

- Schools that respect the "ways of being" of students
- Local school control of the necessary resources; autonomy and local partnership at the schoolhouse
- Permanent ongoing preparation for teachers based on "reflection on practice"
- Transformation of schools into creativity centers where one teaches and learns with joy, ending the practices of grade retention and pushout expulsion
- An entirely new system of assessment appropriate to the children and their life experience
- A new pedagogy where students and their life experiences are the curriculum in constant interaction with teachers who can help them question and explore who they are and what has gone before

Paulo Freire in this *Pedagogy of the City* reignites the concerns and challenges he set forth in the *Pedagogy of the Oppressed*. These dialogues are tempered in the fire of actual administration of the public schools of São Paulo. He nourishes us all in our efforts to make real schooling the birthright of every child.

Part One

EDUCATION
FOR LIBERATION
IN A
CONTEMPORARY
URBAN AREA

· 1 ·

The Deficits of Brazilian Education

It is not possible for any educator who takes on the responsibility of coordinating the work of a department of education, no matter in what city or state, to escape the challenge of the deficits Brazilian education is presently experiencing. Anyone who takes on such a responsibility is faced on the one hand with the quantitative, and on the other, the qualitative issues. For example, one is faced with the inefficiency of schools to address the needs of all school-age children, both those in school and those who remain without schools, and with the inadequacy of the curriculum. It is important also to point out that a critical politics of education cannot mechanically understand the relationship between these deficits—quantitative and qualitative—but it must understand them dynamically and contradictorily. It is impossible to attack one of these deficits without bringing to consciousness the other. If one expands the capacity to understand schools in terms of need, sooner or later there will be pressure towards changing the school profile. If one tries to democratize the schools, from the point of view of their internal structure, teacher-students relations, administration-teachers, and so forth, and their relations with the community within which each is situated, one

searches to change the face of the schools. One grows, necessarily, in the process.

Not only have we constructed more classrooms but we
have also maintained well-kept, clean, joyful-pretty classrooms. Sooner or later the very beauty of the space requires
another beauty: the beauty of competent teaching, the joy
of learning, and the imagination to create. All this occurs
within the context of freedom of action and the beauty of
the adventure to create.

It is fundamental, I believe, to state the obvious: the educational deficits to which we have referred hurt, above all,
the working poor. Among the eight million children without
school in Brazil there are no sons and daughters of families
who eat, dress up, and dream. And even when, from the
point of view of quality, the Brazilian schools do not attend
fully to the so-called children born with silver spoons in
their mouths, the poor children—those who could go to
school and stay there—are the ones who suffer the most
from the inequality of education.

Let's take the here and now about the educational practice
for a moment only; I refer to the evaluation process, the
assessment of knowledge. The evaluation criteria the school
uses to measure students' knowledge—intellectualism, formal, bookish—necessarily helps these children from the so-
called privileged social classes, while they hurt children
from poor and low socioeconomic backgrounds. And in the
evaluation of the knowledge base of children—evaluated
when they first arrive in school and during the time they
stay in school—the mechanism in general never takes into
consideration any "knowledge from life experience" the children bring with them to school. Thus the poor students
are put into a disadvantageous position. The experience of
children from the middle class results in the acquisition of

a middle-class vocabulary, prosody, syntax, in the final analysis a linguistic competence that coincides with what the school regards as proper and correct. The experience of poor children takes place not within the domain of the written word, but within direct action.

By making more democratic the criteria employed to evaluate students' knowledge base, schools should deal more effectively with certain gaps relative to the children's experience so as to help them transcend obstacles in their process of knowing. It is obvious, for example, that children who lack familiarity with written words or who have an infrequent need for writing, both in the streets and at home, will have more difficulty going from oral language to written language. This does not mean, however, that the lack of these experiences develop in these children a different "nature," that determines their absolute incompetence.

A dream I have, among many others, is to sow words that derive from a written social experience in poor and working-class neighborhoods—that is, in areas where memories are preponderately oral. The graffiti writers who embellish this city could very well contribute towards the realization of this same craziness that industrialists and business people could finance.

In Chile, when I lived there during my time in exile, the power of words in areas of agrarian reform were created by the peasants themselves who, in the process of becoming literate, would "plant" words on tree trunks, and sometimes on the dirt ground on the roads. I would like to follow a population of kindergartners involved in a similar project and observe their every step in the process of their experience with literacy.

But, let's return to the beginning of our conversation. On taking over the administration of the Department of Education for the City of São Paulo I could not but be alert to the

deficits that we have been talking about. At any rate, even before thinking about the construction of classrooms or school
units to meet the demand of students—if we were to receive
this year an adequate budget or other extraordinary resources—we would have to confront the enormous challenge
we inherit from the previous administration. About fifty
school buildings were in a deplorable state with ceilings falling, floors caving in, electrical wiring presenting real threats
to life; fifteen thousand school desks were broken, and many
schools were without any desks whatsoever. It is impossible to
ask students from such neglected schools to take care of them.
Not a single principal of all these devastated schools ever
ceased to request help from those who were responsible for
repairing their schools. I plan beginning next March to have
political pedagogical meetings and conferences in the inner
cities where I will show videos recording the sad state in which
we received these schools so as to invite community people to
participate in addressing the care of what is a public domain.

For all this year we plan above all to restore the gutted
schools, while making all possible attempts to provide proper
maintenance throughout the schools systemwide. At the same
time, however, we have begun to work seriously towards the
reformulation of the curriculum in these schools. I have given
Ana Maria Saul, a teacher from the Pontifica Universidade Catolica—one of the the more competent curriculum theorists
in Brazil—the task of coordinating the curriculum reform.

We plan in reality to change the "face" of our schools. We
do not think that we are the only ones capable of doing so
or the most competent, but we do know that we are able
and that we have the political imperative to reform these
schools. We dream of an effective public-school system that
will be constructed step by step within a space of creativity.
We dream of a democratic school system where one practices a pedagogy of the question, where one teaches and

one learns with seriousness, but where seriousness never becomes dullness. We dream of a school system where, in teaching necessarily the content, one teaches also how to think critically.

For us, a curriculum reform could never be something made, elaborated, thought by a dozen "experts" whose final results end up in the form of curriculum "packages" to be executed according to instructions and guidelines equally elaborated by the "experts." Curriculum reform is always a political-pedagogical process and, for us, substantively democratic.

Considering what there is in educational practice of sociology, politics, science, artistic, ethical, social, and communication, we began to construct during January and February groups of specialists, without any strings attached to the Department of Education. These specialists include university teachers of the highest level, with whom we are developing a profound and interdisciplinarily critical comprehension of educational practice.

We have involved in this process physicists, mathematicians, biologists, psychologists, linguists, sociologists, political theoreticians, art educators, philosophers, and jurists involved in human rights programs and, more recently, a team of educators and psychologists who work on sexuality. At the end of this month we will have our first meeting with all these teams when we evaluate the work that has been done up to now. In the beginning of March we will be establishing, throughout the different sections of the Department, a frank and open dialogue with principals, coordinators, supervisors, teachers, janitors, cooks, students, parents, and community leaders. We hope to be able in these encounters to help form and solidify the school community councils.

In a really progressive, democratic, and nonauthoritarian way, one does not change the "face" of schools through the central office. One cannot decree that, from today on, the schools will be competent, serious, and joyful. One cannot democratize schools authoritarily. The administration needs to bear witness to the faculty and staff that respects it and not be afraid to point out its limitations. The administration must make clear that it can make mistakes. The only thing that it cannot do is lie.

Another thing the administration has to do in its dealings with the faculty and staff and their respective roles is to think, organize, and create programs of permanent staff development counting on the help of those scientists with whom we have until now been working. A permanent staff development must be based, above all, on reflection about practice. It is through thinking about his or her practice, it is through confronting the problems that will emerge in his or her daily practice, that the educator will transcend his or her difficulties with a team of specialists who are scientifically qualified. It is clear that none of this can be accomplished from night to day and without struggle. All of this requires a tremendous effort, competence, material conditions, and an impatient patience.

Sometimes I cannot help but to laugh, when certain criticisms leveled against me say that I do not think about anything concrete. Is there anything more concrete than to fight to repair fifty defaced schools? Is there anything more concrete than to think theoretically about curricular reform? Is it vague and abstract to visit as many schools as possible in the district to discuss concrete problems with principals, teachers, students, and janitors?

In finalizing this conversation, I would like to say to the educators with whom I have the pleasure of working that I continue to be ready to learn and that it is because I am always open to learning that I am able to teach as well.

Let's learn while teaching one another.

·2·

To Change the Face of Schools

Escola Nova: In practice, what is the difference between the Workers' Party's[1] proposal in relation to other pedagogical proposals?

Paulo Freire: Even though I am an educator who is a member of the Workers' Party (henceforth PT)—I enlisted as a member of the PT when I was still in Europe—I would not like to give an answer to your question as if I were speaking for my fellow PT members. Without pretending, in any way, to give the impression of personalizing the answer, I prefer to speak about the way I think, convinced that, substantively, I will locate myself in PT's horizon of aspiration. On the other hand, I would not like either to make comparisons, even with myself, between what I think and what I do as a

---

1. The Workers' Party was founded in 1980 amidst the turmoil created by the military dictatorship that had governed Brazil since 1964. The external debt, high inflation and general poverty provided the proper climate to support an intense mobilization of workers in the periphery of São Paulo, under the leadership of metal worker Luis Ignacio (Lulo) da Silva. The political organization of workers had significant backing and success thanks to the participation of leftist intellectuals. The victory of Luiza Erundina, the mayor of São Paulo, is an example.

Workers' Party educator, and the way educators from other parties think and act. I will speak about some issues that I believe are fundamental to the educational politics of a party that, being "popular" (in a progressive sense), is not authoritarian; being democratic, is not democratized; being educationally orientated, recognizes the participant learner of the progressive social movements. The education that such a party must put into practice and refine is just as political and is just as impregnated with ideology as any other that a conservative party may plan and execute.

The very nature of the educational practice—its necessary directive nature, the objectives, the dreams that follow in the practice—do not allow education to be neutral as it is always political. This is what I call the "politicity" of education—that is to say, the quality that education has to be political. The question before us is to know what type of politics it is, in favor of what and of whom, and against what and for whom it is realized. It is for this reason that we can affirm, without fear of being wrong, that, if the educational politics of a progressive party and its practice are the same as those of a conservative party, one or the other is radically wrong. Thus, the great necessity we have as progressive educators is to be more consistent, and to diminish the distance between what we say and what we do. I am not, however, advocating that progressive educators become angels or that we beatify ourselves in our search for absolute coherence. In the first place, an absolute consistency would make life an experience without fragrance, color, and taste; and, in the second place, it would not even allow us to know that we are being consistent, since there would be no inconsistencies to teach us otherwise.

But, what is necessary is the constant yearning, the critical effort to make what is said and what is done more comparable to one another. It is imperative to say again what is said when the practice requires it. What is not possible, for me, is to speak for the downtrodden masses, but, at the same time, I should also take into consideration that these downtrodden masses may not have the sufficient maturity to self-direct; it is as if to speak of a democratic school while hand-tying the teachers, because of their so-called lack of competence, with teaching "packages" that are impregnated with our "expert" knowledge. What is not possible is to negate the practice for the sake of a theory that, in some fashion, ceases in being theory to become pure verbalism or intellectualism. By the same token, to negate theory for the sake of practice is to run the risk of losing itself in the disconnectedness of practice. I advocate neither a theoretic elitism nor a practice ungrounded in theory; but the unity between theory and practice.

Let's take a look at another important point in the role of these considerations. If there is something that a serious progressive educator has in common with an equally serious conservative educator it is that they both have to teach. For this very reason, they both need to know what they teach. But, if we take a close look at what identifies the progressive and conservative educators—in other words, the act of teaching a certain content—immediately we begin to perceive that, from what initially identifies them, we begin also to see what separates them. I do not want to say that four times four equals sixteen for a progressive educator and fourteen for a conservative teacher. What I want to say is that the very comprehension of what teaching is, what learning is, and what knowing is has connotations, methods, and ends that are different for one another. There is also difference in the treatment of objects to be taught and learned so they can be learned by students—in other words, the programmatics of content.

For the coherent progressive educator, the necessary teaching of content will always be associated with a "critical reading" of reality. One teaches how to think through the teaching of content. Neither can we teach content by itself as if the school context in which this content is treated could be reduced to a neutral space where social conflicts would not manifest themselves, nor can the exercise of "thinking correctly" be disconnected from the teaching of content.

It is this dynamic relation, this procedural, that I intend to stimulate in the public schools. Moreover, for a coherent progressive educator it is not possible to minimize, and dismiss the "knowledge from lived experiences," that students bring to school. The progressive educator's knowledge rests in making it comprehensible so that the rupture established by the more exact knowledge, knowledge of a scientific nature, establishes vis-à-vis the students' knowledge. This does not imply that the students' lived experience should be devalued. On the contrary, it is through the knowledge of lived experiences that one reaches the so-called more exact knowledge.

Expanding a little more about these considerations, perhaps I could say that, while in a competent conservative educational practice one searches, through the teaching of content, to hide the raison d'être of a sizable number of social problems, in a progressive educational practice, also competent, one searches, through the teaching of content, to unveil the reasons behind these problems. The first tries to accommodate, to adapt the learners to the world that is given; the second tries to make the students unquietly critical, challenging them to understand that the world that is being presented as given is, in fact, a world being made and, for this very reason, can be changed, transformed, reinvented.

I should conclude this question by saying that progressive educators know very well that education is not the lever for the transformation of a society, but they also know the role that education plays in this process. The efficacy of education rests on its limits. If education could do all or if it could do nothing, there would be no reason to speak about its limits. We speak about them, precisely because, in not being able to do everything, education can do something. As educators of a progressive administration[2] it behooves us as to see what we can do so we can competently realize our goals.

Escola Nova: How did you put into practice the literacy campaign before the military coup d'etat of 1964?

Paulo Freire: I believe it would be interesting to answer this question by referring to the official document that was published after an international conference sponsored by UNESCO, in 1975, in which I participated. The conference was held in Persepolis; thus the document is named "Letter of Persepolis." One of the principal objectives, if not the principal objective of that meeting, was the evaluation of literacy campaigns in different parts of the world. The text underlines the relation between the success, more or less, of the so-called adult literacy campaigns and the social and political transformation process observed or not in the societies within which these campaigns were taking place.

The problem seems obvious to me. It is one thing to implement a literacy campaign in a society in which the subordinate classes begin to take their history into their own hands, with enthusiasm, with hope, and another to put into practice literacy campaigns in societies in which the subordinate classes find themselves removed from the possibility of exercising a greater participation in the transformation of their society.

---

2. Freire refers to the Workers' Party mayoral administration of São Paulo, under which he became the Secretary of Education on January 1, 1989.

In 1964, Brazil had not made any revolution, this is true. We were living a populist experience under Goulart's[3] government. But we also were living a moment of profound unquietness, of curiosity, of the presence of subordinate masses in the streets and parks. The populist model was living its fundamental ambiguity. On the one hand, populism gains its very existence through the manipulated stimulation of the subordinate classes, even though manipulated, on the other hand, it runs the risk of disappearing if the left could make itself viable through the subordinate masses, or if the right, because of the subordinate class's presence, would end the populist feast. It was precisely the latter that occurred. But, the important thing is to consider that, in that short period of time, there was a popular will—it does not matter that it was more for rebellions than for revolution, and also a curiosity. These factors provided the necessary basis for the plans that we coordinated from the Ministry of Education in Brazilia. Today, after many years, the situation is different, even taking into consideration what the victory of the Workers' Party in São Paulo represents in terms of hope in many Brazilian cities.

It seems to me that we should not work in terms of campaigns, the deeper meanings of which suggest something with an everyday character, but to attack the problem without giving the literacy work such an emergency character. On the other hand, to the extent that we confront the literacy problem, here and there, we should from the very beginning try to go beyond literacy, constructing with the subordinate classes progressive alternatives in the area of progressive education.

3. Joao Goulart (1918–76) was vice-president of Brazil under Janio Quadros. Goulart assumed the presidency when Janio Quadros resigned the presidency after six months of an obscure government. Goulart, height of nationalism and heir of

Within the spirit of your question there is something else to be said. In this moment, an interdepartmental team consisting of the Department of Culture, Department of Education, Department of Health, Department of Housing, Department of Social Welfare, and Department of Sports, is working in direct relationship with social movements in the elaboration of projects of popular progressive education. The point of departure of one of these is a participatory research project that will give us a report concerning the wishes, dreams, and aspirations of the population in the area where the research will take place. One of the advantages of this type of work rests on the fact that the very methodology of research makes it pedagogical and consciousness raising. Perhaps just as important, or even more so than the character of the participatory research I have just mentioned, is the effort, the political resolutions that brought these departments to work together. We are confident of this fact.

Escola Nova: What is the percentage of the city's budget that is allocated to education?

Paulo Freire: The budget program that was approved in 1988, and which is in place this year, foresees the application of 27.1 percent of the tax receipt going toward education. In the meantime, from this percentage, 4.6 percent represents costs for the supplementary programs of food and health, which the new constitution determines be financed with other budgetary resources, and 1.7 percent are costs related to the Department of Social Welfare, youth centers and

---

Getulio Vargas, began to nationalize sectors of the economy and state. After two years in office Goulart was ousted in the military coup d'état of 1964.

youth shelters, which have a more assistentialist than educational character. Excluding these costs, only 20.8 percent of the tax receipts are really allocated toward education. It is worth noting that these receipts are only 51.5 percent of the total amount budgeted (35 percent would come from loans).

Escola Nova: What are your goals?

Paulo Freire: I have spoken a great deal, even before taking on the position as Secretary of Education for the city, about our serious desire to change the face of our schools, including kindergarten. In truth we pretend, and for this end we have already begun to work since the first days of our administration to transform the schools into creativity centers, where one teaches and learns with joy. I do not pretend to say, in making this affirmation, that there aren't schools in the school system today where the children do not feel happy. What is necessary, however, is to generalize this climate that, in turn, to be created and maintained, requires the convergence of various factors.

Material conditions, staff and faculty salaries, the maintenance of schools, timely repairs, and streamlining the bureaucracies are all indispensable to the effective functioning of schools. Respect for educators, students, and all others are necessary as well. However, how can we show respect to the children, to the educators, the school administration, cafeteria workers, janitors, parents, and the local community, if the schools are deteriorating day by day, threatening the health and the peace of mind of all, even in view of the insistence from the directors over the course of many months to have the necessary repair work done in their schools?

How can one teach and learn with joy in a school full of puddles of water, with exposed electrical wires, with sewage systems plugged up, bringing about nausea and vomiting? This is the serious problem we are presently confronted with in view of the fifty schools or more that we found in deplorable states. The bureaucratic mechanisms that are there, the endless paperwork—one taking care of the other—the slow pace that characterizes going from one sector to the other, all of this contributes to the raising of obstacles in the serious work we are doing. An administration like the PT's demands a radical transformation of the bureaucratic machine. The one presently in place would even hurt a conservative administration. This perverse bureaucracy annihilates and gags the progressive administration that we wish to create. But we are not going to allow this to continue.

One way, perhaps, to begin to put into motion the transformation I have spoken about is to create what my assistants call "front-line" workers to execute a determined task in a correct and rapid form. We are doing this now with respect to a number of projects and we will create next week one of these "front lines" to confront the question of school repair which will require significantly more money than what we have received. This "front line" will consist of personnel from, at very the minimum, three departments—Education, Public Works, and Finance.

As you can see, we cannot speak of educational goals without making reference to the material conditions of schools. Material conditions are not only "spirit," but also "body." The educational practice whose politics we are charged with developing democratically take place in the concreteness of the school, in time and space, and not only in people's heads.

In the final analysis, we need to show that we respect these children, their teachers, their schools, their parents, and their community; that we respect what is public, treating it with decency. Only then can we expect and demand that everyone respects also the school desks, the school walls, as well as the school doors. Only then can we speak of principles and values. The ethical is intimately tied to the aesthetic. We cannot speak to students about the beauty of the knowing process if their classrooms are flooded with water, if the wind enters, directly and maliciously into the classroom, cutting their not so well-dressed bodies. In this sense, to repair the schools rapidly is already to change their face a little, not only from the material point of view but, above all, from the perspective of the schools' "soul." We need to make it clear that we believe in and respect those who are downtrodden. To repair the schools rapidly is a political act that needs to be lived with consciousness and efficacy.

To change the face of schools implies also listening to the children, to ghetto societies, parents, school directors, instructional coordinators, supervisors, the scientific community, janitors, cafeteria workers, etc. It is not possible to change the face of schools through an act of the secretary's goodwill. To conclude, I would say that we are engaged in a struggle for schools that are competent, democratic, serious, and happy.

Escola Nova: What will you do in view of the high percentage of school dropouts?

Paulo Freire: In the first place, I would like to refute the concept of dropout. The Brazilian poor children do not drop out of school; they don't leave school because they want to. The Brazilian poor children are expelled from school not, obviously, because this or that teacher, for a reason of pure personal antipathy, expels these students or flunks them. It is the very structures of society that create a serious set of barriers and difficulties, some in solidarity with others, that result in enormous obstacles for the children of subordinate classes to come to school. But also, when these children come to school, they experience the same barriers and difficulties in staying in school to acquire the education to which they have a right.

There are reasons, however, internal and external to schools, that explain the "expulsion" and grade retention of children from subordinate classes. We will attack the internal reasons, above all, at the level of the Department of Education by the following: the effective use of school time—time for the acquisition and production of knowledge, the permanent preparation of teachers, and the stimulus of a critical educational practice that provokes curiosity, questioning, and intellectual risk. In this aspect, as with everything that has to do with the school practice, I expect to hear from principals, teachers, supervisors, and pedagogical coordinators. I wish to hear their suggestions in reference to minimizing the school negativity that contributes towards the "expulsion" of students. Already now in March,[4] fifteen days after the reopening of classes, I will begin, first, to visit schools two mornings per week, not as the one who waits, with certain eagerness to inspect[5] so as to punish teachers or other servants who are not doing their jobs, but as someone who finds it a duty, while secretary, to collaborate with those who battle in the trenches. Second, I will meet in a systematic manner, whenever possible, with teachers, instructional coordinators, principals, supervisors, cafeteria workers, and janitors.

---

4. The school year in Brazil begins, in general, at the end of February or in the beginning of March, depending on the school level.

5. This is an ironic allusion to Janio Quadros, the mayor who preceded the Workers' Party administration in the city of São Paulo. In his need for self-affirma-

The expulsion and grade retention themes will be always treated in search of solutions or realistic and effective paths. Once more, we recognize that, no matter how competent that we may be, we can not do it all.

Escola Nova: What changes do you propose to introduce in the school curriculum?

Paulo Freire: In answering an earlier question, I spoke of our efforts to change the face of the schools. To change the face of schools is to struggle to make a progressive school. To do so necessarily involves a curricular change. No one, however, in a democratic manner, can change the school curriculum from Monday to Tuesday. When it is done in an authoritarian manner, from top to bottom, along the wishes of enlightened specialists, the curriculum transformation, beyond the construction of an unacceptable contradiction from the point of view of the PT's administration, is not efficient.

There are two things that I think I can now say. The first is that, in general terms—and now I have to repeat myself— we dream of schools that, being serious, nonetheless should never become dull. Seriousness does not need to be over-bearing. The lighter the seriousness the more effective and convincing it is.

We dream of a school that, because it is serious is dedicated to a form of competent teaching, a school that also generates happiness. What there is of seriousness, even painful, work-intensive, in the process of teaching, learning, and knowing does not transform this task into something

tion as an administrator, Jánio, in a dictatorial manner, would make surprise visits to schools and other sectors of government to punish possible wrong doing.

sad. On the contrary, the joy of teaching-learning should accompany teachers and students in their constant yearning for joy and knowledge. We need to remove the obstacles that make it difficult for happiness to envelop us and never accept that teaching and learning are necessarily boring and unhappy practices. It is for this reason that in the earlier answer I noted that the urgent repair of schools already represented a move towards changing the face of schools, from the point of view also of their "souls."

We dream of a school that is in reality democratic, that attends for this very reason, to the interests of underprivileged children and that, as rapidly as possible, will diminish the reasons in its womb for the "expulsion" of children from subordinate classes.

The second thing that I can say now is that, during the entire months of January and February we worked in the School Department with teams of specialists, physicists, mathematicians, psychologists, sociologists and political scientists, linguists and humanists, philosophers, artists, jurists, and specialists in sexuality. We analyzed different movements of the educational practice—the epistemological, the political, the cultural, the linguistic, the aesthetic, the ethical, the philosophical, and the ideological questions in meetings with these specialists, teachers from the Pontificia Universidade Catolica de São Paulo, the University of São Paulo, and from the State University of Campinas, who have been contributing their time without any strings attached.

The twenty-seventh of this month we will have the first plenary interdisciplinary meeting during which we will evaluate the work finished up to now and discuss the participation of these scientists in the next phase—in which we will begin our dialogues in school centers and in the neighborhoods in which they are situated.

The seminar with students from the fifth series that we should have in March is part of this process. Just like the one we will carry out in the East Zone[6] listening to representatives of grassroots movements. There will be follow-ups to these meetings with principals of schools, teachers, coordinators, etc. Our intention is to make a dialogue possible between grassroots groups and educators, between grassroots groups and students, educators of the school system and the scientists who come to us.

At this moment this is what I can tell you in reference to your question.

Escola Nova: And with respect to the teacher training?

Paulo Freire: We all know that the preparation of teachers has been neglected. One of the central preoccupations of our administration could not have been other than the continuous preparation of teachers. One can not think of changing the face of schools; one can not think of helping the schools become serious, rigorous, competent, and happy, without thinking about the permanent preparation of teachers. For us, the continuous preparation of teachers will take place whenever we can, preponderantly, through reflection on practice. Whenever possible, and I hope that we do not wait too long in initiating this process, we will bring together, with competent specialists, teachers who work with children's literacy. The dialogue will take place around the practice of teachers. Teachers will talk about their problems, their difficulties and, in the reflection on the practice they speak about, there will emerge a theory that informs practice.

---

6. February 1989, the date of this interview.

The reflection on practice will be the central focus, but it does not exhaust the forming efforts. Other activities will be programmed. In this week that is beginning, I will be creating another "front line" of workers to help me program the process of teacher preparation.

Escola Nova: What changed in your life after you became the Secretary of Education in the city of São Paulo?

Paulo Freire: Obviously my day-to-day routine changed. Before I lived quietly between my bedroom, my library, my academic activities, and my family. Once in a while, I attended an international congress, a conference. I would give interviews to magazines and national and international newspapers. I would take trips within and outside Brazil. Now the rhythm is different. The challenges are different.

The difficulties are great. Nothing, however, discourages me, makes me regret having accepted the mayor's invitation. It is a pleasure for me to accept the duty to all I can do alongside an excellent, competent, and untiring team of educators.

I have learned a great deal in this first phase of experience. After two months in the department, dealing with an illogical and threatening bureaucracy, I can say: It's worth it!

· 3 ·

A Pedagogical Project

Psicologia: What is the pedagogical project being implemented by the City's Department of Education in Mayor Luiza Erundina's administration?

Paulo Freire: There are no neutral administrations or pedagogical projects. Mayor Luiza Erundina's administration, then, would not become an exception to this rule. The fact that her administration is markedly directed towards needs and interests of the underclass segment of the population, however, does not mean it would turn its back on those segments of the population who, for living a good, comfortable life, don't always know what it means just to survive. It is interesting to observe, however, how those who live the good life tend to consider those who simply survive as incapable, uncultured, envious, dangerous, marginal, and to consider what in the city is beautiful and well cared for as their own property. For them, those who survive make the city ugly. Erundina thinks right. She doesn't think like that.

We could reflect in the same terms upon the pedagogical project we are committed to developing at the City's Department of Education. We want a progressive public-school system, not a demagogically populist one, which rejects elitism but does not show anger towards children who eat and dress well. We want a truly competent public-school system: one that respects the ways of being of its students, their class and cultural patterns, their values, their knowledge, and their language—a school system that does not assess the intellectual potential of lower-class children with evaluation tools created for those whose class conditioning gives them an undeniable advantage over the former.

How can one tell a poor boy who "didn't do well" on a given series of tests that he does not have a sense of rhythm, when he can dance the samba excitedly, when he can sing and accompany his bodily rhythm with the drumming of his fingers on a match box. If the test for such an evaluation were to demonstrate the ability to dance the samba while marking the rhythm with a match box, my grandson would possibly be considered incapable in relation to the results obtained by a poor boy or girl. We must make it clear, though, that the school system we want does not intend to be unfair to children of the more favored classes, neither does it intend to deny lower-class children, in the name of defending them, the right to study and learn what the former learn because what they study is "bourgeois." The creation, however, of a school system like this requires, in the broadest sense of the word, the reformulation of its curriculum. Without this curricular reformulation, we won't be able to build the public schools we want: serious, competent, fair, joyous, and curious—a school system that transforms the space where children, rich or poor, are able to learn, to create, to take risks, to question, and to grow.

Even before I took office at the Department of Education, I had started working towards that, living what was a first stage of my reflections about this curricular reformulation. This reflection was intensified in January and February, when I met with a group of specialists of the highest level, professors from the University of São Paulo, from the Pontificial Catholic University of São Paulo, and from the State University of Campinas, to discuss theories of knowledge and education, art and education, ethics and education, sexuality and education, human rights and education, sports and education, social classes and education, language and education. It is important to emphasize that these intellectuals, physicians, mathematicians, biologists, sociologists, philosophers, art-educators, etc., who now amount to a hundred, have been making excellent contributions without any burden to the Department of Education. We have recently had the first meeting with all of these specialists, in which we discussed some hypothetical experimental projects in the area of curricular reformulation. It is important to say that, by no means, could we think of extending to schools—whose daily life, whose world of affective, political, and pedagogical relations constitute for us the fundamental terrain for pedagogical practice and reflection, the results of our bureau studies to put them into practice. For political conviction and pedagogical reasons, we refuse the "packages" with recipes to be followed word for word by the educators who are at the base. For this reason, in the following stages of the curricular reformulation process, we will be speaking directly with principals, teachers, supervisors, cafeteria workers, mothers, fathers, community leaders, and children. It is necessary that they talk to us and tell us how they see the schools, how they would like them to be, that they tell us something about what is and what is not taught in school and about how it is taught. No one can democratize the schools alone from the secretary's bureau.

Psicologia: What is, in practical terms, the most adequate or effective way to conduct this educational project for children and for adults in the public school system?

Paulo Freire: As I just said, we will never impose on the public-school system a profile of schools, no matter how much it may express our political option and our pedagogical dream. Especially because we reject authoritarianism and licentiousness, manipulation and spontaneity, and because we do not act in a spontaneous or licentious manner, we do not exclude ourselves. Quite the contrary, we accept the fact that there is no reason why we should try to escape the duty of intervening, of leading, of ensuing, always acting with authority, but also respecting people's freedom and dignity. For us, there cannot be a more adequate and effective way to conduct our educational project than the democratic route, than the open, courageous dialogue. I believe the meetings I have already had with all of the principals in the public-school system revealed the real political resolve with which I come to the meetings. I am equally sure that this political resolve will become clearer and clearer in my weekly visits to schools, when I talk to all about the pedagogical life of the schools. With time, it will be proven that political clout cannot be used to serve some at the expense of others. In reality, we cannot even think about gaining teachers' compliance with, for example, a model of teacher/student relationships that is more open, more scientific, and also riskier by imposing our point of view onto them. We need, above all, to convince, almost convert. The permanent development of teachers, which necessarily had to receive

emphasis in our project, is one of the opportunities to overcome certain misunderstandings or errors that constitute a
barrier for the effective implementation of our project.

Psicologia: Considering that your pedagogical project has an
explicit political and ideological character, how is education
being treated in relation to information or content from the
sciences and from erudite culture?

Paulo Freire: It is not a privilege of our ongoing pedagogical
project to have an explicit political and ideological character.
Every pedagogical project is political and filled with ideology. The issue is to determine in whose favor or against
whom educational politics, which is a necessary component
of education, is constructed. In response to your question,
it seems important to talk about the impossibility, at all
times, of having an educational practice devoid of content. I
mean, devoid of an object to be taught and learned by the
educator, so it can be learned by the learner. This is due to
the fact that educational practice is naturally epistemological
and that it is not possible to know nothing unless nothing is
substantiated and becomes the object of knowledge, thus
becoming content. The fundamental issue is politics. It has
to do with which content gets taught, to whom, in favor of
what, of whom, against what, against whom, and how it gets
to be taught. It has to do with what kind of participation
students, parents, teachers, and grassroots movements have
in the discussion around the organization of content (curriculum design). This is exactly one of our major concerns,
as I have mentioned before, the effort we make to reformulate the curriculum in the public schools of São Paulo.

For us, there is no doubt about the right lower-class children have, proportionately to their age levels, to be informed

about, and formed according to, the advances of science. However, it is indispensable that, in becoming progressive, the school system know and value the knowledge of class, the experience-based knowledge the child brings to it. It is important that the school respect and accept certain progressive methods for knowing things, which are almost always at odds with scientific patterns, but which lead to the same results. It is necessary that, as the system becomes more competent, the schools also become more humble. All socially and historically produced knowledge has historicity. There is no new knowledge that, once produced, can be presented as unsurpassable.

It is necessary that the progressive schools, especially those located in the deepest areas of the city periphery, seriously consider the issue of language, of the syntax of the underclass, which I have been talking and writing about for so long. This issue has been so long and many times misunderstood or distorted. I'll take advantage of a certain dimension of your question to return to the subject. It is not possible to think of language without thinking of the concrete social world we constitute. It is impossible to think of language without thinking of power and ideology.

What does not seem fair to me is that the schools, grounded in the "standard patterns" of the Portuguese language, continue, on the one hand, to stigmatize the language of the low-class child and, on the other, to interject in the child a feeling of incapacity, from which one is hardly freed. I have never said or written, however, that poor children should not learn the "standard pattern." For that it is necessary that they feel their identity respected and that they not feel inferior for speaking differently. Finally, it is necessary that, as they exercise their right to learn the standard patterns, they realize that they should do it not because their language is ugly or inferior, but because by mastering the so-called standard patterns they become empowered to fight for the necessary reinvention of the world.

Psicologia: In what ways do your ideas converge to or diverge from the CIEPs developed by Darcy Ribeiro in the Department of Education of Rio de Janeiro?

Paulo Freire: I have great respect for and a great friendship with Darcy Ribeiro, an intellectual for whom loving, imagining, dreaming are not antagonistic to the seriousness and rigor of science.

I don't think about how the project we are implementing here converges with or diverges from the CIEP's. Since you asked the question, I'd like to make it clear that it is impossible to think about the educational practice, thus the school, without thinking about the issue of time, of how to use time for the acquisition of knowledge, not only in terms of the learner-educator relationship, but in terms of the whole, daily experience of the child in school.

The serious, progressive school system cannot waste the time a child has to learn. But it seems to me that one can only think of how to use time in a productive manner starting from a minimum limit of time. This minimum period of time, it seems to me, should be four hours. I cannot see how one could work efficiently in three-hour shifts, for example, except in emergency cases. In these cases—at the moment we are experiencing such cases—it is necessary that we make it clear to the parents the reasons behind the shortened school day. The issue of time is placed in the core of the conception of CIEP's, which in and of itself gives them undeniable credit.

For the city of São Paulo, I would rather do the best we can to live intensely, productively, and creatively the four hours of activity in elementary and middle schools.

Psicologia: How do you deal with the expectations of the school clientele (students and parents), who can react with opposition or indifference to the pedagogical proposals of the present Department of Education?

Paulo Freire: Also in a democratic way. We should be starting this March, in inner city areas, pedagogical rallies and assembly meetings where we will, on the one hand, show the dismal state in which we found some fifty schools and, on the other, discuss the steps we are taking towards changing the "face" of the school. Still this month, we will have a first meeting with forty to fifty fifth graders to hear from them what they think about school and to tell them a little about how we think.

There will obviously be those measures we'll take because putting them into practice is our responsibility. But everything that needs to be discussed will be.

Psicologia: What is expected from the community Educational Councils in relation to the quality of teaching?

Paulo Freire: In a way, the answer to this question is included in the previous one. The pedagogical assemblies or plenaries, we hope, will play a fundamental role. Through them, it is possible to have the deep, real participation of communities, parents, and representatives of grassroots movements in the whole life of schools.

I have said, and I repeat, that the democratization of schools can't be made as the result of a voluntarist act of the Secretary of Education, decreed from his bureau.

· 4 ·

Educational Workers' Questions

Union: Who is Paulo Freire in the present Brazilian educational context?

Paulo Freire: I wouldn't feel comfortable talking about myself and placing myself within the present Brazilian educational context. All I can say, without falling into pitiful immodesty or into the even more pitiful false modesty—a "shameless" form of being immodest—is that I have been a vibrant educator filled with life, present within the Brazilian educational context. That is enough for me.

Union: What does it mean to be an education worker in Brazil today?

Paulo Freire: There isn't an education worker, in Brazil or any other society, who is an abstract concept, a universal concept. The education worker, as such, is a politician, regardless of whether he or she is aware of it or not. It seems to me that it is essential that every education worker, every

44

educator, assume, as rapidly as possible, the political nature of his or her practice. That he or she define himself or herself politically. That he or she make his or her option and be coherent about it. In this sense, what it means to be an education worker in Brazil today depends on whether your political, your ideological position, is clear or unclear; whether you are progressive, in this or that direction; whether you are conservative or reactionary; or whether that is due to naïveté or conviction.

It is not easy to draw a profile of the progressive educator, or of the reactionary one, without running the risk of being simplistic. Positioning myself among the progressive educators of Brazil today, I would say that assuming this position means to work conspicuously for the public schools, for the raising of teaching standards, for the dignity of teachers, and for their permanent development. It means to fight for progressive education, for the increasing participation of the underrepresented classes in community, neighborhood, and school councils. It means to motivate the mobilization and organization not only of your own professional class but of workers in general as a fundamental condition for the democratic struggle leading up to the necessary and urgent transformation of Brazilian society.

Union: How are the public schools doing?

Paulo Freire: The reactionary powers within this country have harmed the public schools. The educational policy of the military governments was oriented towards the privatization of education, which necessarily implied undeniable contempt for public education and a corresponding disregard for teachers. Obviously, the policy of education privatization would directly affect the interests of underrepresented

classes, who would, once again, pay for the comfort and per-
quisites of the so-called favored classes.

It is interesting to observe the trajectory a given generation can draw upon enrolling in any elementary grade in
the country. First of all, we should consider the frightening
number of school-age children who "stay" out of school. In
reality, they don't stay out of school, as if staying out or going
in were a matter of choice. They are kept from entering,
just like, further along, many of the ones who manage to
get in are forced out, and these are referred to as if they
had dropped out (willfully). There is no dropping out of
school. There is expelling. Secondly, we should consider the
number of underclass children who manage to get in or who
are not kept from entering the public school and compare
this to the number of those who manage to pass from the
first grade on to the second and from that to the third. Let
us also think about the underclass youths who go through the
so-called equivalency programs very precariously, attending
night classes, which for the most part are not free of charge.

These same generation middle-class boys and girls go
through their primary and secondary education in rigorous
private schools, and when the time comes to enter college,
they take special review classes in the content areas before
taking their entering exams. At this point, those students
who were able to pay for private schools enter the free federal and state universities. The few poor youths who managed, with great effort, to finish their secondary education,
unable to compete with the others, have no recourse other
than going to expensive private colleges, which often lack
any rigor.

The public-school system is not doing very well, not because it is its nature not to be well, as many would like it to
be and imply. Again, we should emphasize that the public

school system isn't doing well on account of the deep contempt the dominant classes in this country have for anything that even smacks of the people. That is why I emphasized in the previous answer the need to fight for the public schools and progressive educators.

Union: How do you see the decentralization of education all over the country? Aspects: privatization of education, political favoritism, double standards in human resources management, quality of teaching, "crooked" decentralization.

Paulo Freire: Whenever I think about decentralization, what motivates me and makes me in favor of the process is exactly what there may lie in it (which we should fight for) of the democratic, of the decentralizing, of the antiauthoritarian. For me, sometimes correct, valid arguments lose their validity because they are raised against the process itself, when they should be directed against distortions of it, which confuse decentralization with lack of governmental obligation towards education. Sometimes, people talk about decentralization as if it had some sort of immutable nature that would necessarily create or stimulate, for example, authoritarianism on the level of political struggle or an antidialectical and myopic view of education. In reality, authoritarian and favoritist policies are not waiting for decentralization to come into existence. Nor is the antidialectical, myopic view.

On the other hand, the argument that towns are not competent—I mean, do not have people competent enough to manage their own education, culture, health, etc.—isn't valid either. It is obvious that towns have needs and deficits, but it is also obvious that, once they have to face their difficulties, they will overcome them: only by confronting these difficulties will towns be able to move ahead. What it would necessarily take is effective cooperation from the central government and from state governments, as well as a policy of exchange among towns.

In a society like ours, where authoritarianism cuts across social classes (among us, the arrogant academic who looks down on others is just as authoritarian as the porter who guards the teachers' room door on the last day of classes in a university), every effort in favor of democratic practices is important.

Union: Is there anything in the presently established formal school that can be of use?

Paulo Freire: Yes. The grading system, for example. The vertical and horizontal integration of content, the coeducation on all levels. It is urgent, however, to overcome the college-preparatory-course nature of the grading system—primary education as preparatory for secondary education and this one preparatory for higher education.

Each stage of education should propose a kind of "plenitude" within itself so that those who only completed the elementary stage, successfully, felt capable of moving ahead with their acquired knowledge, without experiencing the frustration of having undergone preparation for something that didn't happen.

Union: Is the transformation of society impacted by education? To what extent?

Paulo Freire: I have been saying, for a long time, that education is not a lever for the transformation of society, but that it could be. The fact, however, that it isn't even though it could be does not diminish its importance in the process.

This importance grows when, in the democratic practice, progressive parties reach the government and, with it, a share of the power. In this case, everything that can possibly be done, with competence, to introduce democratic change in the school structure must be done. There must be, for example, permanent development of educators, without ideological manipulation, but with political clarity, making clear the progressive orientation of the administration. Other changes are: curriculum reformulation, community participation in school life, parents' associations, school councils, etc.

If the bourgeois school is only concerned with the authoritarian teaching of content, hiding, in the process, the reasons behind facts or talking about false reasons, in the school of a progressive government it is crucial that the teaching of content be accompanied by a critical and revealing reading of reality. Finally, only within a dialectic understanding of the school-society relationship, is it possible not only to understand but also to develop the fundamental role of school in the transformation of society.

Union: How do you see the full-time school?

Paulo Freire: A few days ago, in another interview, I was asked a similar question. I'll allow myself, once again, the right to repeat myself a little. It doesn't seem possible to me to consider educational practice without including the issue of time, of how to use time to acquire knowledge, not only in the teacher-student relationship but also in the whole daily experience of the child in school. In an excellent master's dissertation, Professor Eliete Santiago, from Pernambuco, who is the present Secretary of Education of Cidade do Cabo near Recife, recently drew a lucid analysis of the use of time in school works against children who come from subordinate groups.

The serious, progressive school cannot waste the child's time to acquire knowledge. But only from a minimum time limit for the school practice, it seems to me, is it possible to think about how to use it productively. For me, this minimum is four hours. I can't see how it would be possible to work efficiently in three-hour shifts. In this sense, a school formally referred to as full-time could waste time, from the point of view discussed here. The designation full-time, in and of itself, can't operate miracles; it is necessary to know what to do with the time.

Union: What is the role of an educator aware of reality and who knows he or she is an ideological agent?

Paulo Freire: I think the role of a consciously progressive educator is to testify constantly to his or her students his or her competence, love, political clarity, the coherence between what he or she says and does, his or her tolerance, his or her ability to live with the different to fight against the antagonistic. It is to stimulate doubt, criticism, curiosity, questioning, a taste for risk taking, the adventure of creating.

Union: Tell us about the schools of São Paulo and what the Workers' Party (PT), in the city administration, has planned for them?

Paulo Freire: I can tell you something about the schools of the São Paulo public school system. There are 654 schools. From those, we received fifty-five in deplorable state. Ceilings falling apart, huge puddles in the classrooms, exposed electric wires, clogged sewers, threatening rats—in spite of the complaints made by principals since the beginning of last year. A dismal situation.

But, if these calamitous conditions are only seen in fifty-five of the schools, that does not mean, by any means, that the others are all in excellent shape. They all require immediate repairs and maintenance so they don't become equally damaged.

We received the public school system of São Paulo in a state that revealed the abuse of an administration that not only took poor care of public property but also intimidated and abused the conscience of educators, and, in fact, *all* school employees. Erundina found the city in debt, construction works suspended, contractors' projects suspended. In the Department of Education, besides struggling physically to reconstruct the schools (without money), we, loyal to the option of our party, have had to start thinking about educationally reformulating the school system, changing its face. In order to do that, we'll have to reformulate the curriculum; we are already working on that. Because of that, on the other hand, we also have to rethink the administration, improve the channels of communication between its various sectors, putting them all at the service of the school, which is the fundamental space of the Department where the pedagogical practice takes place.

We are all engaged in the struggle for a competent municipal public school system, where children can learn—living—that studying is as serious as it is pleasurable.

· 5 ·

Challenges of Urban Education

Terra Nuova: How do you see the situation of Brazil today—on the one hand, the development which makes Brazil a great economy, on the other, the poverty which so harshly punishes the majority of the population?

Paulo Freire: I don't believe anyone with minimum sensitivity in this country, regardless of political position, can live in peace with such a cruel, unfair reality as this. One thing, though, is to feel bad, and immediately find such whiny arguments as "the people are lazy," "the people are uncultured," "Rome wasn't built in a day," to explain the tragic situation and to defend purely self-serving hypotheses of action; another thing is to be taken by "just rage" and engage in political projects for substantive transformation of reality.

My sensitivity makes me have chills of discomfort when I see, especially in the Brazilian northeast, entire families eating detritus in landfills, eating garbage; they are the "garbage" of an economy that boasts about being the seventh or eighth economy in the world. My hurt sensitivity does more, however, than just give me chills or make me feel offended as a person, it sickens me and pushes me into the political fight for a radical transformation of this unjust society.

My hurt sensitivity makes me sad when I know the number of poor boys and girls of school age in Brazil who are "prohibited" from entering school; when I know that, among those who manage to get in, the majority of them are "expelled," and people say they "dropped out." My lashed sensitivity makes me horrified when I know that the illiteracy rate among youths and adults has been increasing in the last years; when I realize the contempt with which the public school system has been treated; when I verify that, in a city like São Paulo, there are one million boys and girls living on the streets. But, together with the horror that such a reality provokes in me, there is the necessary anger and the indispensable indignation that, combined, give me courage to fight democratically for the suppression of this scandalous offense.

Terra Nuova: Tell us about your development as an educator: how did it begin; the time of the dictatorship; the exile. Why did you accept the assignment for the Municipal Department of Education?

Paulo Freire: Nobody becomes an educator on a Tuesday at four in the afternoon. Nobody is born an educator or marked to be one. We make ourselves educators, we develop ourselves as educators permanently, in the practice and through reflecting upon the practice.

It is true that we have, since childhood, certain likes and preferences, certain ways of being, or of saying and doing things that, sometimes or almost always, coincide with the nature of certain crafts like education, for example. That is why, sometimes, in light of these likes and preferences, adults will say about boys and girls that they were born doctors, educators, or artists. In reality, however, nobody is born ready.

I was a boy with many pedagogical adumbrations, a certain curiosity, an eagerness for knowing, a taste for listening, a desire to speak, respect for the opinion of others, discipline, perseverance, knowledge of my limits.

My career as an educator started exactly in my experience as a student, when one way or another, those likes and preferences were stimulated, accommodated, or denied. Still very young, shortly after I began middle school, I started to "teach" the Portuguese language. And through teaching my students grammar and syntax, I started to prepare myself to understand my role as a teacher. If, on the one hand, this role was not to propose that my students re-create the whole history of the content I taught them, on the other hand, it was not just to lay out a profile of it either. The fundamental thing was to challenge the students to realize that learning that content implied learning it as the object of knowledge. The issue wasn't to describe those content concepts but to unveil them so the students could relate to them with the radical curiosity of those who search and who want to know. It is true that, back at the beginning of this discovery of teaching, to which corresponds an understanding of the dynamic and critical nature of learning, it wasn't yet possible for me to talk about it as I do now.

This epistemological certainty that learning the object, the content, presupposes the apprehension of the object, the realization of its reason for being, accompanies me in every step of my practice and of my theoretical reflection over practice. It accompanied me in my experience as a young, almost adolescent, Portuguese teacher, in my work along the streams and on the hills of Recife, at the beginning of my youth, as a progressive educator, in the formation of the fundamental principles of the so-called Paulo Freire Method (a designation I don't like), in my activities as a university professor, in Brazil and abroad, and in the present effort for the permanent professional development of educators in the public school system in which I am involved as Secretary of Education of São Paulo, together with the excellent team I work with.

To be more objective in answering your question about my progress as an educator, maybe I could make reference to moments and people who, directly or indirectly, marked me.

The hardships I lived in my difficult, if not tragic, childhood, and the manner in which my parents behaved in coping with those difficulties, were both important in my development as a person, which preceded my development as an educator, without any dichotomy between them. My father's death—when I was thirteen; the trauma of his absence; my mother's kindness in her struggle to put me through school; the figure of an excellent educator from Recife, Aluizio Araujo, the father of my second wife, Ana Maria (or Nita as I call her), to whom I owe the privilege of studying for free in his school; some teachers whose example I still remember today; the beginning of my studies at the Law School of Recife, when Elza, an extraordinary woman and educator, came into my life; also her loss, which almost took me as well, had it not been for another woman no less extraordinary, Nita; ten years of political and pedagogical experience with urban and rural workers in Pernambuco; my academic work, essential readings; a certain camaraderie with Christ and with Marx, which surprises certain Christians and makes naive Marxists suspicious. All these are the ingredients that necessarily permeate and define my progress as an educator. And they are followed by the equally important impact of the rich and challenging exile experience. This exile resulted from a theoretical understanding of education as a political act, of education as a process of discovery, of the democratic education founded on the respect for the learner, for his or her language, for his or her class and cultural identity, also, an understanding of the theoretical explanation for the defense of an education that reveals, unveils, that challenges; above all, the exile resulted from the putting into practice of such an understanding of education. It was that practice that frightened, in the sixties and still does today, the dominant, authoritarian, and perverse classes. It was the putting into practice of such an education that took me to prison, away from the university, and finally to the almost sixteen years of exile.

The opportunities I had to grow, to learn, to reevaluate myself in the exile were such that sometimes Elza would humorously and wisely tell me, "You should telegraph the general who responds for the Presidency of Brazil to thank him for the opportunity they afforded you to continue learning." She was right.

In the almost sixteen years of exile, I lived in three different places: Santiago, Chile; Cambridge, Massachusetts; and Geneva, Switzerland. From there, I roamed the world as a tramp of the obvious. I taught courses and seminars, participated in conferences and congresses, assisted revolutionary governments in Africa, in Central America, and the Caribbean; I helped liberation movements, ran risks, made friendships, loved, was loved, learned, grew. And while I did all that and "suffered," in the sense of incorporating what I lived and did, I never stopped considering Brazil as a preoccupation. Brazil never was for me a remote, bitter memory.

The Brazil of my preoccupation was exactly the Brazil subjected to the military coup, picturesquely called "Revolution of 64" by its executers. It was the silenced Brazil, with its progressive intellectuals expelled, with its working class manacled, with men like Helder Camara, the prophetic archbishop of Recife and Olinda, threatened and silenced. All the well-lived time, however, of exile becomes preparation for the comeback. So in June of 1980, we returned to Brazil permanently, settling in São Paulo.

In a first stage, I dedicated myself to what I called relearning Brazil. I visited the whole country again. From north to south I spoke, above all, to youths curious about what we had done before 1964. I feel that I still have an obligation to write about this. I don't know when or whether I'll do it. I went back to being a teacher. I became a professor at the Pontifical Catholic University of São Paulo and at the State University of Campinas. I also wrote, but mostly, I spoke a lot in those years. Still in Europe, I became a founding member of the Workers' Party (PT), in whose administration of São Paulo I am now the Secretary of Education. That was the first time I became affiliated with a political party, with card, name, and address. Everything right. Everything legal. The reason was that, for the first time in this country, a political party was born from down up. The Workers' Party wasn't born rejecting the so-called intellectuals for being intellectuals, but rejecting elitist and authoritarian intellectuals for claiming ownership over the truth of the working class and of the revolution. And, since I have never accepted this type of arrogant intellectuals, I felt comfortable, from the very beginning, as a modest militant member of PT.

And why did I accept being the Secretary of Education of São Paulo?

First of all, because I am secretary of PT's administration, and in particular, within Luiza Erundina's administration. In other words, because I can say, on TV programs, on the radio, and in the newspapers, that at the Department of

Education, political clout and political connections cannot surpass anybody's rights. Secondly, because, if I had not accepted the honorable invitation by Erundina, I would have to, for a matter of coherence, pull all of my books out of press, stop writing, and be silent till death. And this was much too high a price. To accept this invitation was to be coherent with everything I have ever said and done; it was the only way to go.

I did accept the position, and I am pleased because I did.

Terra Nuova: Talk a little bit about the Paulo Freire Method—Conscientization or Literacy? How do you position yourself in relation to the criticism you receive in that respect?

Paulo Freire: Maybe the best way to address the question you pose is to insist that every reading of the word is preceded by a reading of the world.

Starting from the reading of the world that the learner brings to literacy programs (a social and class-determined reading), the reading of the word sends the reader back to the previous reading of the world, which is, in fact, a rereading.

Words, sentences, articulated discourse do not take place up in the air. They are historical and social. It is possible, in cultures with primarily or exclusively oral memory, to discuss, in projects of progressive education, the greater or lesser extent to which the subordinate group's reading of the world at any given time is a critical one, without the reading of the word. What does not seem possible to me is to read the word without a connection to the learner's reading of the world. That is why, for me, the literacy process with adults necessarily implies the critical development of the reading of the world, which is a political, awareness-generating task. What would be wrong, and what I have never suggested should be done, is to deny learners their right to literacy because of the necessary politicization there would not be time for literacy in the strict sense of the term.

Literacy involves not just the reading of the word, but also the reading of the world.

Terra Nuova: What are your guidelines as Secretary of Education, and how do you see them in the context of PT's administrations?

Paulo Freire: I am convinced, and this is quite obvious, that progressive administrations like PT's cannot be distant from and indifferent to the issue of progressive education. They are administrations that need to face the issue of the prestige of the public schools, the struggle for their improvement, which in turn is connected to a profound respect for educators and for their permanent development.

The issue of adult and youth illiteracy is related to the quantitative and qualitative deficits in our education. There aren't enough schools to serve the peoples' demand—eight million children in Brazil are out of school—and the education offered is elitist, removed from the expectations of the subordinate classes.

Every year there tends to be a higher number of illiterate youths and adults, on the one hand, because millions are kept from entering school and, on the other hand, because those who fail end up being expelled from school. Therefore, when addressing the issue of illiteracy, it is pressing:

a. That we do it without the remedial nature literacy campaigns usually have. It is important, then, to think about how to incorporate literacy students into the regular educational system.

b. That we fight:

   i) to overcome the quantitative deficit of our school and

   ii) to overcome the high rate of failure through adequate and efficient teaching in the basic school.

None of this can be done overnight, but it will be done one day.

Terra Nuova: How do you view the role of nongovernmental organizations of cooperation in Europe in relation to PT's administrations?

Paulo Freire: I always view organizations of cooperation in a good light, be they European or not, so long as the relationships established between them and us, PT's administrations, are relationships of mutual respect, dialogical relationships, through which we can grow together, learn together. On the contrary, I will always see negatively any so-called organization "of cooperation," which distortedly, however, intends to impose its options onto us in the name of the help it might give us. In reality, there are no neutral organizations of cooperation. For that reason, they should also be very clear about the administrations with which they seek relationships and for which they study cooperation projects.

We demand very little to live well with any organization: only that it treats us with respect.

·6·

Youth and Adult Literacy

ICAE (International Council For Adult Education): How would you describe the universe of the marginal population targeted by the International Year for Literacy?

Paulo Freire: In São Paulo, the majority of the illiterate population is made up of migrants coming from the poorest states in the north, the northeast, and also from the country-side of São Paulo and Minas Gerais. In general, these are people who make a living off odd jobs or unskilled professions (i.e., construction workers' aides, cleaners, housekeepers). Therefore, their level of income is very low, not even enough to satisfy basic needs like food and housing. They often live in slums, overcrowded tenement houses, and in the self-made shacks in the outskirts of São Paulo. They spend large portions of time commuting and do not take advantage of the recreational areas and services that the city offers (which are usually centralized and not free). Some exceptions are: going to Se Square or Ibirapuera Park on Sundays, or most recently, the Carmo Park (East Zone). A large part of the illiterate population is made up of women, who have a doubled work load.

ICAE: Many people are criticizing the International Campaign for Literacy and asking: Why should people learn how to read and write when they have no food or housing, which is the case for most of the illiterate?

Paulo Freire: We believe that we should advance to a more global view—not partial—of social rights and of social movements. The social movements themselves, especially after the discussions around the Constitution,[1] became more aware of the fact that the various problems are interconnected and that it is important to fight for the real gain of the many social rights that still only exist on paper in our society. It is important to note that, for us, since work for literacy leads to a more critical reading of reality, it constitutes an important instrument for recovering citizenship, which reinforces the citizens' engagement in social movements that fight for better standards of living and social transformation.

ICAE: In your opinion, what can possibly be done within the time frame of the campaign year?

Paulo Freire: We believe it is possible to create a wide debate with the different sectors of civilian society: schools, universities, unions, and especially the mass media in order to involve the whole population, thereby pressuring the governmental sectors responsible for the problem. We also be-

---

1. The present Brazilian Constitution (1988) was written by a Constituent Congress elected in 1986.

lieve it is possible to create or participate in events that make an inventory and analysis of what has been done in Brazil and, especially, to participate in events where proposals for minimizing the problem can be raised and presented. On the level of the City of São Paulo, in 1990, we intend to initiate the Literacy Movement (MOVA) of São Paulo, together with grass-roots groups who already develop literacy projects, and with other sectors, such as churches and universities, who may come to join this effort to create two thousand literacy centers serving more than sixty thousand people. Thus, we have defined the following general objectives for the MOVA Project:

1. To reinforce and expand the work of popular groups who already work with adult literacy in the outskirts of the city.
2. To develop a literacy method that enables students to think critically.
3. Through the Literacy Movement to contribute to the development of political consciousness in the students and teachers involved.
4. To stimulate grassroots participation and the struggle for the social rights of citizens, emphasizing the basic right to public and progressive education.

ICAE: How should literacy students be involved in the campaign?

Paulo Freire: By having their expectations heard, by presenting proposals, evaluating the existing experiments (official or unofficial). In that respect, it is of fundamental importance that various sectors—universities, unions, and especially the media—make room, open channels for the students to express themselves. I think this should be one of the main concerns and initiatives during the campaign year because so far, only educators, and literacy specialists have participated in events concerning literacy. I believe it is time for the learners to take the floor.

ICAE: What role can the ICAE take in the Literacy Movement?

Paulo Freire: I believe that the ICAE should, above all, function to stimulate and give incentive to broad and individual actions around the literacy issue in other countries. Besides, it can contribute to the systematization and socialization of various initiatives, thereby facilitating a more fertile exchange among different countries.

ICAE: What could you tell the one million people who cannot read or write about literacy in order to motivate them to become literate? In other words, how can literacy help them obtain housing, food, and work?

Paulo Freire: Illiterate individuals, especially those living in the big cities, know better than anyone else how important for their lives as a whole it is to be able to read and write. However, we cannot encourage the illusory notion that literacy alone can solve their housing, food, and work problems. These living conditions will only be altered through the collective struggle of the working class for structural changes in society.

In sum, I think it would be important, during our work for the International Year for Literacy, to insist on and fight for the continuity of this effort in time and in the struggle for the construction of public and progressive education.

· 7 ·

History as Possibility

Eloi Lohmann: How is the pedagogy of the oppressed possible today, given that the present reality of Brazilian education is totally different from that of the early sixties?

Paulo Freire: It seems obvious to me that the question does not refer to the book *Pedagogy of the Oppressed,* but to a certain understanding of education that is committed to the necessary emancipation of the oppressed classes.

There are a number of aspects to be considered in reflecting about this topic. We could discuss, for example, the implementation of the pedagogy of the oppressed within the Brazilian school system, at the elementary, secondary, or higher levels. We could think about material obstacles—budget, the physical layout of schools—as we could think about those that have a more ideological nature (without being less material), with which we are confronted when trying to implement an education in favor of people's emancipation. We could still discuss the same effort for such an educational practice outside the school system, within the realm of informal education, or we could also analyze the barriers that are raised in opposition to a kind of social commitment.

I believe that a statement of general order can be made: the pedagogy of the oppressed, not the book I wrote, but the understanding of education in favor of the permanent emancipation of human beings, whether considered as a class or as individuals, constitutes a historical question (of what to do) in relation also to historical human nature, which is finite and limited. Precisely because the pedagogy of the oppressed is historical, takes place in history, and is being lived by historical beings who, in a way, transform themselves while realizing it, the forms of implementation of this pedagogy, as well as that of the oppressor, vary in time and space. There is one aspect that I consider to be of fundamental importance in regard to the practical implementation of the pedagogy of the oppressed. I am referring to the need felt by the progressive political, pedagogical leaderships to detect the level on which the struggle has been taking place in this or that society. It is these levels that explain the "present state" of education here or there.

In conclusion, any effort for democratic education in favor of the underrepresented classes would meet enormous obstacles both in the sixties and today. Today, however, we would respond to it differently. I am talking about the authoritarian and elitist ideology that puts a mark on and stifles us. While authoritarian elitism or elitist authoritarianism are typical of the reactionary educator, they become the negation of the progressive educator. In the sixties, like today, progressive educators were forced to narrow the distance between "advanced discourse" and the authoritarian and traditional practice.

Eloi Lohmann: How do you see your journey, and that of

education itself, from Recife to the world and now to São Paulo?

Paulo Freire: No educator can consider his or her professional progress indifferent to or in spite of the pedagogical ideas of his or her time or space. On the contrary, he or she proceeds on the journey, challenged by these ideas, which he or she combats or defends. One denies, affirms, grows, immobilizes, grows old that way, or is always young. These ideas, on the other hand, are not the ones that make up the educator's historical, cultural, and material world. They express social struggles, the advances and regressions of history, but they also constitute active, powerful agents of change in the world. There is a dialectical relationship between the material world that generates the ideas and the ideas that can influence the world by which they are generated.

Obviously, I could not escape that. More than the dramatic, tragic nature of the Northeast where I was born and grew up, the profound exploitation of subordinate classes, the perversity of the dominant classes and existing social structures, the silence imposed on the subordinate classes, to which was added the reinforcement of an authoritarian education, restricted to book learning—all that showed me a way to follow as an educator and, therefore, as a politician. It was the way to an education that denounced oppression and announced liberty, the way to a pedagogy of indignation. From Recife to exile, from exile to Brazil again, during all this time moving about, this has been my commitment. And because this is the commitment to a future built upon a changing present, I learned along the way that the fundamental condition to be able to keep going is to be always open to learning. Curious and open to the new—this is how

I have been able to comprehend more than I expected in the last five months as the Secretary of Education of the City of São Paulo. By becoming reacquainted with the known and getting to know the unsuspected, in these last months my life has been a succession of days when almost nothing goes unnoticed by me. In reality, this has been a painful time and an intensely pleasurable one, like every time of discovery and creation, of making and remaking.

Eloi Lohmann: You have always been a consultant to revolutionary projects in education, but you have not had the power (of state) for very long. How is this relationship processed— the relationship of your pedagogical proposal with you as the power? The Board of Education of the City of São Paulo is an administrative structure of reasonable size. How does the process for a new political and pedagogical dynamics operate alongside highly bureaucratic state mechanisms?

Paulo Freire: It seems to me that I should begin responding to your question by placing one of your statements—that is, that I am now in power—in a relative perspective. Strictly speaking, I am integrating the government of the City of São Paulo, in charge of its Board of Education, which, in fact, gives me some power but not *the* power. This does not mean, in any way, that I have now less power than I had before. I have more than I had before, but a lot less than one might naively think I do. In reality, we are a progressive government that cannot do everything it dreams of.

At any rate, I do not see a contradiction in the fact that today, as Secretary of Education, I try to carry through some of the proposals or put into practice some of the ideas for which I have been struggling for so long. I try to use the power derived from being a part of the city's government to, at least, realize part of the old dream that moves me: the dream of changing the outlook of schools; the dream to making schools democratic; the dream of overcoming authoritarian elitism, all of which can only be done democratically. Can you imagine trying to overcome the authoritarianism of schools authoritarily?

One of the good things about the democratic game is that it is not enough to be convinced of the correctness of your ideas or your practice. You have to demonstrate that this is the case and convince those who oppose your ideas and practice of their validity. I would even say that, in many cases, you need to convert the opposition. Besides, it is not a contradiction to try to concretize old political and pedagogical aspirations in the city's Bureau of Public Education. I find this type of battle joyful.

Of course, it is not easy. There are all sorts of obstacles slowing down transformative action. Piles of paper taking our time; administrative mechanisms blocking the development of projects, deadlines, time limits: it is a total mess. In fact, this bureaucracy even gets in the way of the dominant class, but after all, the dominant class ends up adjusting the bureaucracy to its own interests. The hard thing is to have this bureaucracy at the service of the progressive dreams of a people's government, rather than a populist one.

Eloi Lohmann: In practical terms, what sets PT's pedagogical proposal apart from the others?

Paulo Freire: I wouldn't like to make any comparisons between our ways of viewing the administration of education and of public assets in general and that of other parties. I would, however, like to highlight some important points for us, the PT administration. One of them is what we mean by participation. For us, participation cannot be reduced to the sole cooperation that different segments of the population should and could give to the administration. Participation, or cooperation, for example, through the so-called *mutiroes* (state-community improvement initiatives where the community provides the manpower), used to repair school buildings and child-care facilities, to clean streets and parks. Without denying the importance of this kind of cooperation, for us participation should go further. For us participation involves a more active presence of the subordinate classes in history, instead of their mere representation. It involves the political participation of the popular classes, through their representations, on the decision-making level, not just to carry out preplanned projects. The authoritarian understanding of participation obviously reduces it to a presence of the popular classes in the administration conceded only at certain moments. For us, then, local school councils are extremely important, for they constitute a real level of power in the creation of a different school system. Popular participation, for us, is not a slogan, but the expression of the city's accomplishment of democracy and the way to it.

The more firmly we consolidate the democratic practice of participation, the further away we will be moving, on the one hand, from antidemocratic, elitist practices and, on the other, from the no less antidemocratic grass-roots practices. I realize it is not easy to implement projects or experience community and grassroots participation as a government program and as a political ideal. Above all, it is not easy on account of authoritarian traditions, which we need to overcome, and this cannot be done solely through the discourse contradicted by authoritarian practices.

Part Two

REFLECTIONS ON THIS EXPERIENCE WITH THREE EDUCATORS

· 8 ·

School Autonomy and Curriculum Reorientation

Ana Maria: What were the most important structural changes introduced in the pedagogical model of city-run schools? Do you think they were enough?

Paulo Freire: So far, the most important structural changes introduced in the schools have been focused on school autonomy. With the reenactment of the Common Statute of Schools, approved by the State Board of Education in 1985 and banned by the previous administration, the councils elected in late March this year gain decision-making power. It is up to these councils, especially, to approve the school planning and to prepare the school budget. In order to broaden this participation even more, in decision making and actions, the City's Department of Education, with the support of the City Union of Secondary Students, has initiated the formation of student associations in schools. However, the greatest advance with respect to school autonomy was in allowing individual schools to develop their own pedagogical projects that, with the support of the administration,

73

can accelerate the transformation of the school. Although these changes represent an advance, I consider them to be only the beginning of what I imagine the transformation of the schools should be.

Ana Maria: You are an advocate of the permanent professional development of teachers. Which training and in-service programs for teachers have already been implemented?

Paulo Freire: One of the principal programs in this administration to which I am deeply committed is that of permanent development of educators, because I understand that educators need a serious and competent political pedagogic practice that responds to the new outlook of the school system we seek to build. Six basic principles guide the educator-training program of this department:

1) The educator is the subject of his or her practice; it is up to the educator to create and recreate this practice.
2) The educator's training should give him or her the tools with which to create and recreate his or her practice based upon reflections on his or her daily routine.
3) The educator should be in constant, systematic training, for the educational practice is always in transformation.
4) The pedagogic practice requires an understanding of the genesis of knowledge itself, in other words, an understanding of how the discovery process takes place.
5) The educator training program is a stepping stone for the process of curriculum reorientation of the school.
6) The educator training program will have as its basic axes:

- the outlook of the desired school, as the horizon of the new pedagogical proposal;
- the need to provide basic formative components to educators in the different areas of human knowledge;
- the acquisition, by educators, of scientific advances that may contribute to the quality of the desired school.

This program takes on multiple and varied forms. The training carried out in the school itself, with small groups of educators or with larger groups resulting from the grouping of nearby schools, will be favored. This work consists of following—reflecting upon—the action of educators who work in the schools. It involves explaining and analyzing the pedagogical practice, raising themes of analysis that require theoretical substantiation, and reanalyzing the practice in light of the theory.

Several actions have already been concretely carried out. I would highlight the work of training groups with child educators, coordinators, principals, and teachers, who work with literacy. Training actions have been implemented with pedagogical coordinators within the system. I made the effort to meet personally with educators (principals, pedagogical coordinators) and with all the teachers in large areas of the city (South Zone and North Zone) to explain the pedagogical policy of this administration.

Ana Maria: You have set out to seek the support of professors in universities to the city's educational project, without cost to the City. Which affiliations have already been obtained and what specific contributions have already been made?

Paulo Freire: Right at the beginning of this administration's term, I started to work with university professors from different fields, whom I invited to discuss the proposals for school change. I believe universities have a responsibility toward the other levels of education, and they have a fundamental contribution to make as regards the understanding of knowledge, the prospects of advance in different areas of knowledge, and the formation of professionals who operate within the educational system.

I also believe the approximation between the university and the school would allow the university itself to gain a knowledge of reality that would help it reassess its teaching and research.

In sum, I consider this exchange to be beneficial both to the university and to the city's public schools. The meeting with the presidents of PUC–SP (Pontifical Catholic University—São Paulo), USP (University of São Paulo), and Unicamp (University of Campinas) was extremely profitable. Besides giving us a warm reception, they showed similar intentions in relation to the exchange. We could count on the professionals of those universities, who have been working closely with the Department of Education, specifically within the curriculum Reorientation Commission, participating in the preparation of the curriculum Reorientation Movement, which will be launched on August 21 and 22.

The university professors also developed, during the first semester, important seminars. Some of the themes they explored were: Language, Education, and the Training of Teachers; Curriculum Integration and Education; Ethics in the Process of Curriculum Reorientation. These seminars have been recorded and will be carefully analyzed since they help the building of a critical screen necessary to assist the transformation of the schools. In order for this work to move ahead and expand, the city's Department of Education has signed a specific agreement with USP on the 8th of this month (August 1989), and soon it will sign a similar agreement for technical cooperation with PUC–SP and Unicamp.

Ana Maria: You have always seen the "dialogical relation" in teaching, the incorporation of the student's worldview into the educational process, as a priority. How has the student's participation been made concrete?

Paulo Freire: Having the "dialogical relation" as a priority generates respect for the student's culture and for the valuation of knowledge the learner brings to school. Thus, work initiated from the student's world view is, doubtlessly, one of the fundamental axes upon which teachers' pedagogical practices should be built. This proposal is very serious and profound because student participation should not be understood in simplistic terms. What I propose is a pedagogy that starts from the knowledge the learner brings to school, which is an expression of the social class learners belong to, and which surpasses that knowledge, not in the sense of nullifying it or superimposing other knowledge on it. What we propose is that the knowledge the school works with be relevant and meaningful to the learner.

This should not and cannot be done through depositing information in the students. That is why I repudiate the "banking pedagogy" and defend a critical, dialogical pedagogy, the pedagogy of the question. The public school I desire is one where there is great emphasis on the critical apprehension of meaningful knowledge through the dialogical relation. It is the school that stimulates the student to ask questions, to critique, to create; it is the school that seeks the collective knowledge, by articulating critical, scientific knowledge through world experiences. I would like to say that this type of work is not common practice in the Brazilian schools today. Therefore, it is necessary to invest heavily in the permanent development of educators, in order to reverse the present situation and initiate work where the dialogical relation can happen for real, I mean, as I understand it. I have tried to discuss these aspects in the meetings I have had with teams working directly with teachers and also in pronouncements I have made about the educational policy of this Department, in this administration. It is not possible to say that this proposal has already been concretely implemented, however, I can assure you the actions of this Department are and will be focused on establishing this perspective as the main transformation of the school.

Ana Maria: You mentioned, a few years ago (December 1982), that schools have to reflect the needs and expectations of the population in relation to schools and that teachers are the interpreters of these expectations. What has been done to enable the people to voice what they want from schools?

Paulo Freire: I still say the people have needs and expectations from schools. Schools and the teams working on different levels of the City's Department of Education must know these needs and expectations and take them into consideration in the process of transforming the schools.

Two main actions have been implemented by this Department in order to learn what the population wants from school, as well as the criticisms they have. The first action was to create a school council with decision-making power in every school. These councils must be active and participate in all school decisions and projects. The second action is the creation of the pedagogical plenaries. These are large meetings that take place on Saturdays between Department officials of various levels and the communities. In the first semester two of these plenaries were held. One gathered community members from the East Zone, and the other met with those from the more central areas of the city. Besides these two major events (recorded on video), I have gladly accepted invitations from schools, from the Centers for Educative Action, and from the population itself to meet with various communities.

Ana Maria: Shortly after you took office, you said that there weren't enough spaces in the city's public schools and that it wasn't possible to build as many schools as necessary. You, then, had the idea of turning other empty spaces into schools (churches, for example). How many students could be placed with this measure and what spaces have been used? What is the preliminary evaluation of this initiative?

Paulo Freire: In order to serve all of the children in São Paulo who are out of school for lack of space we would need 546 new buildings. In this administration, there has been an increase in enrollment of 6.39 percent in all regular programs of primary and secondary education and adult equivalency programs. On the one hand, the Department made a serious commitment to use the idle classrooms in schools, especially at night. On the other hand, seventeen community classes of Child Education have been created, which function with the equipment and infrastructure from different sectors of civilian society: conference rooms of unions, churches, community associations. I would like to emphasize that, this month, the Department is taking over 960 classes of Adult Education, which means serving twenty-six thousand new students. Forty percent of these 960 classes will be held in community sites (like the above) other than in the existing school buildings. I accept this solution as a transitory one and as the only viable one, for the moment, in order to expand the service. However, I make a commitment to give these classes my attention in the sense of providing them with all the necessary administrative and pedagogical support in order to ensure quality education for the students. In those terms, I consider the experience a positive one.

Ana Maria: Do you believe you have been able to improve the salaries of teachers and other employees of the City's Department of Education? Do you think they are satisfied?

Paulo Freire: Salaries had a real increase in the first four months of this administration (until April 1989). The increase was 300 percent in relation to the minimum wages paid in December 1988. It was not possible, from May to June, to maintain the salary increases in the same progression, given that the budget was overburdened with the repairs that were necessary in schools. This month, however, the minimum salary to be proposed to teachers will go from NCz$337.00 to NCz$ 701.26. This means that São Paulo has the highest minimum salary for teachers. From September on, salary adjustments will be made monthly, according to the Dieese index. We know that, in Brazil today, except for a very small portion of the population, workers in general have unsatisfactory salaries, which are corroded by inflation resulting from an economic policy that exclusively favors the dominant class.

Ana Maria: What do you think has changed in the Department of Education in relation to the previous administration?

Paulo Freire: Above all, what I think has been changed is that, in this administration, there is a democratic perspective added to the pedagogical policy adopted. The struggle against elitism and authoritarianism are the main goals of this administration. However, I think the teachers and employees would be better suited to answer this question. I suggest that you ask them.

Ana Maria: What are your plans for the next six months? What do you consider as priorities?

Paulo Freire: For the next six months, these are my goals:

- To continue the administration through councils, trying to implement the ideas of representativeness and participation.
- To expand the work of the Department with the Regional Planning Centers and to intensify the pedagogical plenaries, allowing for wider participation of the organized population in educational decisions.
- To initiate, together with schools, the work for Curriculum Reorientation, by organizing discussions with all educators in the public schools, beginning on August 21 and 22.
- To expand the autonomy of schools with the decentralization of the budget, by passing on to the schools more funds which can be managed by the schools themselves.
- To stimulate schools to become more pedagogically autonomous, allowing them to develop their own work plans and projects which can improve the quality of education.

- To implement Integrated Curricula in ten schools (with guaranteed later expansion to the others) until the end of this administration. This work will count on the support from the Centers for Educative Action, from the teams of the Office of Technical Orientation of this Department, and from the university professors.
- To establish priorities in attending to the unserved population, and to locate funds, human resources, and necessary materials.
- To develop a variety of permanent professional development programs, prioritizing those for literacy specialists and elementary and middle-school teachers.
- To hire (through selective examinations) administrative assistants and teachers on levels 1 and 2.
- To continue the construction of eight new schools.
- To continue renovation work initiated in thirty-nine schools in the first semester.
- To provide schools with desks and other basic materials necessary for school work.
- To encourage the development of and to give support to School Councils and free Student Associations.
- To continue to participate in interdepartmental projects within the Administration, to ensure an integrated action of the different branches of government.
- To organize actions leading to the launching, in 1990, of the MOVA–São Paulo project that will aim at significantly decreasing the number of illiterate students in the city of São Paulo.

In sum, there are many plans that, combined, will focus on the transformation of the school system and on the permanent professional development of educators.

·9·

Education at the End
of the Century

Moacir Gadotti: Paulo, the Ministry of Education of Portugal has sent a set of questions, the answers to which it would like to have read by young Portuguese teachers. In sum, these questions aim at evaluating your present ideas, the contemporariness of your method, your philosophy for the construction of education in the society of the future. You have stated that, "the capacity (power) of love is fantastic." The Ministry of Education of Portugal asks: What is the pedagogical dimension of your understanding of love? How do you "futurize" your strategy within a highly technological society? How do you see the contribution of the educator today for the construction of a society imbued with solidarity?

Paulo Freire: I believe that one of the good things a youth, an adult, and an elderly individual can do (all of us have as a historical task the assumption of our time) is to become integrated with, involved in his or her time (historical moment). In order to do that, however, I would remind the

83

young that it is also necessary to assume their time with clarity and to understand history as possibility. Men and women make history from the starting point of given concrete circumstances, from structures that already exist when they are born. However, this time and this space have to be a time-space of possibility, not a time-space of mechanical determinism. What I mean by this is that, the minute I can understand history as possibility, I can also understand its impossibility. The future is not preset. When a generation comes to the world, its future is not predetermined, preestablished. On the other hand, the future isn't, for example, the sole repetition of a present of dissatisfactions either. The future is something that is constantly taking place, and this constant "taking place" means that the future only exists to the extent that we change the present. It is by changing the present that we build the future; therefore, history is possibility, not determinism.

Moacir Gadotti: Now, if history is this possibility, if I assume my own time, I have to discover the fundamental tasks of this time. What should we say to the young teachers who will make the education of the future?

Paulo Freire: Obviously, I could not have the pretense to tell them what their tasks should be, but I can tell them which tasks I have taken on as my own and which have been the tasks of my generation. I believe the most fundamental task that we have at the end of this century, and which has become much more clearly understood at the end of the century, is that of liberation. I wouldn't even say it is the task of liberty. I believe liberty to be a natural quality of human beings. I would even say, more radically put, that liberty is part of the intrinsic nature of life itself, be it animal life, be it plant life. A tree that grows and bends itself seeking the sunlight has a movement of liberty, but a liberty conditioned to its species, to a vital impulse only. It is somewhat different from animal freedom. Today, we ask ourselves about the task of liberation as the restoration of liberty, or as the invention of a liberty not yet allowed. So, I believe this has been a permanent task, a historical one. I wouldn't say it is the biggest task, or the only one, but it is the central task to which many others will be added. I think it is essential that, in understanding history as possibility, teachers also discover education as possibility, in the sense that education is profoundly historical. When we understand education as possibility, we come to realize that education has limits. It is exactly because it is limitable and limited, ideologically, economically, socially, politically, and culturally, that education gains efficacy. Thus, I would say to the educators who are eighteen years old today, and who will, therefore, enter the next century at the beginning of their creative life, that they should be convinced of the efficacy of the educational practice as an essential element in the process of recovering liberty, even if they recognize that education in the next century won't be the key to the transformation of the concrete for the re-creation, the recovery of liberty.

Moacir Gadotti: When referring to the future as possibility, the young of today speak less of sociological categories and more of ethical and anthropological categories. They are categories related to love, friendship, transparency, and political will. The education being born by this generation talks a lot about life, singularity, body. The body becomes a concern that is recovered in a progressive fashion. It seems that the struggle for liberation in some past generations did not focus as much on the body as it did on society. This generation wants to make liberation with pleasure, with love, with the body. How do you see that? I think your pedagogy has placed a high value on the singular, the person, the individual in this struggle. I believe that, for this reason, your ideas are even more contemporary today than they were in the past, because of this search for singularity. You emphasize each individual's contribution in the process of the transformation of history. I would like you to comment on that.

Paulo Freire: I would like to apologize to the readers of this book because what I am going to say may seem a little too humble, but it is strictly connected to your commentary. As the analyst that you are, you said that you feel that some of these ideas, or the essence of this pedagogy itself, are met with even greater receptivity today. It is true. I have recently been in the United States and realized once again that it is no coincidence that the *Pedagogy of the Oppressed* is in its twenty-seventh printing there, and in its thirty-fifth in Spanish. This has to do with what you were talking about. You make a very clear statement; you accept and embrace a certain type of understanding of the world, of struggle. It is clear that you not only are receptive to this view of the body, but also understand the role of the body. In a recent qualification examination (for hiring purposes), I saw how excited you were with the work of one of the applicants in relation to the issue of the body, emphasizing, however (and you did that very well), that one's body is what he or she does, or better yet, that what one does is his or her body. What I think is fantastic about all this is that mine is a conscious body only because I am active; I do things; I think. The importance of the body is indisputable; the body moves, acts, rememorizes the struggle for its liberation; the body, in sum, desires, points out, announces, protests, curves itself, rises, designs, and remakes the world. Neither of us is here to say that transformation can be achieved through an individual body. No, because the body is also socially constructed. Though, it so happens that it is extremely important. And its importance has to do with a certain sensualism. I confess: I do not believe in a revolution that denies love, that puts the issue of love within parentheses. In that respect, I am "Guevarian," Che-Guevarian. Love and revolution go together. There is a lot of sensualism contained by the body and made explicit by the body, even in connection with cognitive ability. I think it is absurd to separate the rigorous act of knowing the world from the passionate ability to know. I am passionately attracted not only to the world but also to the curious process of learning about the world.

Moacir Gadotti: Paulo, what has been communicated to the young, especially through the media, is that being revolutionary is to be grouchy, ugly, boring, stale. This is the idea of revolution which is communicated; how revolutionaries—

Paulo Freire: "—make love with their pajamas on."

Moacir Gadotti: Exactly. This pedagogy we want to construct with the young who will make a new pedagogy, with the young who, soon, will also be writing their books and constructing a revolutionary pedagogy that will certainly not be a stale pedagogy.

Paulo Freire: It might even go back to being that, but I don't believe it will. For example, look at Georges Snyders, the great French educator who, for me, is one of the best expressions of a serious concept of pedagogy at the end of this century. He is a socialist who clearly opts for Marxism and who shows creative loyalty to the Marxist thought. His last book, *La Joie à l'Ecole* (Joy in school), is a hymn to joyfulness. He invites the educator to generate joy through education. The school he describes, the school of his dream, is filled with excitement, but not a less serious one. In Snyders, that would be absurd. It would be absurd to imagine that he could be defending the lack of seriousness. I agree with you; this new generation who reads us today won't build a lax pedagogy, the pedagogy of permissiveness. But I think that the task of liberty, the task of liberation, the history as possibility, the understanding of the conscious and sensual body, full of life, necessarily demands a pedagogy of contentment. I am reminded now, as I make my comments, of the time when I was in Cuba participating in some seminars that pleased me immensely. There I met a young professor of Marxist ethics from the University of Havana who gave me a text about love written by herself, which discussed love from the Marxist ethical point of view. She had presented her text to the young students at the University of Havana, and she told me that they demanded, in their debate with her, that love be made explicit: they wanted freedom to love and to love in order to become free. The young women, for example, complained about the lack of courtship on the part of men in love relationships. They demanded more affection, a certain playfulness with love and affection. So I think, Gadotti, that, firstly, love and affection do not weaken the seriousness of studying and of producing at all. Secondly, I don't think they can, in any way, be an obstacle to political and social responsibility. I have lived my life with love.

Moacir Gadotti: I see from your comments that we are already living the end-of-the-century education, which is an education that fulfills its primary goal, reproduction and construction of knowledge, within a new perspective. The traditional school insisted that one could only learn through effort, punishment, spanking. Today, on the contrary, the young demand charm and beauty, integration between what they study and their lives. They rebel against authoritarianism. But isn't this exactly what the Greeks called *paideia*, (integral education) and Marx called "omnilateral education?" In reality, the construction of the education of the future sends us back to the past, to something original it had in the beginning. Except that, today, it takes on a much more social connotation than it did in Greece, where it was markedly individualistic. Today it is integrated into the joyful construction of the collective. Please, allow me to pose another question: the public school we want to build is not an extension of the bourgeois school to all, because we know that this bourgeois school is elitist and, therefore, it cannot be extended to all. That is why we talk about a progressive public school, i.e., a school for all, with participatory and democratic management and a new quality. How do you see the birth of this school today? How do you view this process of the new emerging from the old?

Paulo Freire: I see that as one of the curiosities of time or one of the reasons for certain curiosities of time. I'd say to the youth who will have access to this interview that, in throwing themselves into the adventure of this serious, rigorous, joyful school, they should never neglect the serious act of studying, that they should never confuse this joyfulness with that of the not-doing. This way, they can prove that the traditional school was wrong about that too; it isn't necessary to harden the desks more than their wood makes them naturally hard; it isn't necessary to harden the children's posture; it isn't necessary to dress the children in collars and ties (so they become taken by a certain suffering, the suffering of knowing) in order to make them learn. No. But, on the other hand, it is important not to be too lax so the child won't lose him or herself just in play and joy. Knowing is a difficult process indeed, but the child has to learn that, because it is difficult, the process of studying becomes beautiful. I also think it would be wrong to tell the child that there is a joyful compensation for the act of studying. It is important that the child realize, from the beginning, that studying is difficult and demanding, but it is pleasant from the beginning.

Moacir Gadotti: Exactly, Paulo, what George Snyders says in his book *La Joie à l'Ecole,* is that there is no separation between the cognitive and the affective domains. He demonstrates that the late twentieth-century educator, as we mentioned, is able to realize practically this dialectical unity, which the traditional educator is unable to do.

Paulo Freire: And that certain new pedagogies can't either because they exacerbate the fun, the affectiveness, at the expense of cognition.

Moacir Gadotti: I believe that traditional pedagogy couldn't realize this fact because it was only at the beginning of this century that the sciences of education became more developed and demonstrated how determining the affective domain is in constructing cognition. Traditional pedagogy couldn't count on the weapons of knowledge that were only developed after the pedagogy of the New School: the act of knowing as natural as the act of walking, of feeding, of loving, etc. Therefore, it separated affective from cognitive, and, thus, relied too heavily on discipline. In the proportion that learning became something external to the habitual context, it was necessary to discipline the students so they could learn. Obviously, without polarizing, the act of studying demands, from the very beginning, a discipline that is part of it, a discipline that propels it and without which the student can't study. However, this is, by no means, a discipline that victimizes. This is what must be made very clear.

Moacir Gadotti: As of January 1, 1989, you have been the Secretary of Education of one of the largest cities in the world. What are you doing for this education of the future. You are an educator. Why?

Paulo Freire: Besides being a great challenge and responsibility, taking over the Department of Education of São Paulo represents an opportunity to try to put into practice a number of proposals that I have dreamed of, written about, and discussed for a long time. I consider, however, that the ideas I have been presenting and advocating, both in my writing and through my performance as a teacher in Brazil and abroad, are shared with progressive educators who wish for a democratic, responsible, serious public education. Thus, I have referred to the need to transform the "face of school" in this administration, because I am sure this school that expels students (while calling it "school evasion"), that reproduces the marks of authoritarianism of this country, that has blocked parents' and communities' access to the school does not have a "face" that can be either liked or maintained. However, it is necessary to understand that this transformation can't be accomplished in a day, or as fast as I would like it to be. That is because my option of how to implement the change involves listening to all the others who make up the school (parents, students, employees, educators, the communities where it is located, and the specialists in different areas of knowledge). And this is not a simple technical or administrative job. I believe that, since the beginning of this administration, I and my working team have initiated a great action in order for this change to happen. This isn't, however, an accomplishment that can be completed in six months. The greatest obstacle in the way of improving the schools' pedagogical work has been the extraordinary effort required to implement repairs to a physical infrastructure that has been totally scrapped within an extremely small budget left by the previous administration. From all the schools in generally precarious conditions, forty-nine were in such bad shape that they had to be partially closed for repairs, in order not to put the students, teachers, and employees at risk. I also found a deficit of thirty thousand desks, which forced many students to watch their classes standing or sitting on the floor. This is unbelievable, when we think that we are in the city of São Paulo, and it denotes extreme contempt for education and public property. Added to the difficulties is the ineptitude of the administrative machinery. In some cases, the necessary resources for certain actions is available, but the red tape is so intense and makes everything so slow and complicated, that it seems to have been created just to stop certain actions from being implemented.

I would like to insist, however, that the schools we wish for won't be born from the simple enactment of a decree, especially because this would be an authoritarian position that could not guarantee improvement. Transforming the schools in the right direction will involve serious and profound work with educators, touching on ideology, the making of commitment, and teachers' professional development. Although implementing this kind of change is what would bring the most obstacles, I don't consider such obstacles to be insurmountable.

Moacir Gadotti: Paulo, a last question, at the request of the Ministry of Education of Portugal. In a technologically advanced society, how do you see the importance of all this for education?

Paulo Freire: I am convinced that the Department of Education of São Paulo has made one more step in the direction of bringing this city to the standards of our times. I am talking about the Central Laboratory for Educational Informatics (Computer technology), which we opened last August and will prepare the first teachers to function as monitors in schools for the implementation of Project Genesis. Our goal, until the end of the administration, is to set up computers in all public schools to help the teaching-learning process.

I think education can't be reduced to technology, but it can't be done without it. The way I see it, it is impossible to start the next century without finishing this one first. I believe that the use of computers in the teaching of our children can expand, instead of reducing, their critical and creative capabilities. It depends on who uses them, in favor of what or whom, and for what purpose. We have already given schools the essentials; now we can give them computers. After all, we need to overcome the underdevelopment Brazil faces in relation to the First World. We haven't come to the Department of Education to watch the death of schools and education, but to push them into the future. We are preparing the third millennium, which will demand a shorter distance between the knowledge of the rich and that of the poor.

· 10 ·

Lessons from a Fascinating Challenge

Carlos Torres: I would like to begin by asking Paulo Freire about his past. How did you become involved in the field of education? Where did you start to live and write *Pedagogy of the Oppressed*?

Paulo Freire: In the first place, I should say to those who will see us on this video, hear us and read us—and also to you—how happy I am to have the opportunity to speak to hundreds of people with whom I may never come into contact and whom I may never meet personally. At any rate, however, to speak to and with people is always a cause for great joy. I may also add, that my present happiness is enhanced by the fact that you are mediating this conversation.

Now, I will attempt, little by little, to answer your question. I have, in fact, some reasons for liking this first question because, in its totality, we can perceive that, for you, (as well as for me) no one is born as an educator as no one is born as a medical doctor, engineer, or teacher. We become medical doctors, engineers, or teachers. What happens with many of us—influenced by our environmental conditions—is that, from our early childhood, we almost always reveal ourselves in our preference for certain toys and games, in the representations of our fantasies, in the unveiling of some of our desires, certain tastes, certain inclinations, certain attitudes that point to a possible educator in us, a possible artist, or a possible medical doctor. This happened to me. When I was a child, as far as I can remember, I had certain tastes, some inclinations, some desires that announced my predisposition to becoming the teacher I am today. This does not mean that these tastes were not also experienced by many other people and that many children who had similar predispositions did not necessarily become teachers later on. Adverse conditions can atrophy these predispositions along the way.

I was, for example, very curious—in general all children are curious—but, for me, the curiosity was always something very alive in my very being, always waiting for the least challenge to trigger my total involvement in questions, investigations, and doubts. Sometimes, when I think of that short space of time of my life, I have the impression that my entire body was always very curious. I was always asking questions and not always of my parents but also of myself. I always liked to go beyond the answers given and generate new questions from them. I also remember how I used to take risks, not in adventures that exposed me to bodily harm but in risks that involved appreciation of objects, defense of my tastes, and the affirmation of myself.

I was not born a teacher, as I mentioned before. But the taste for curiosity, my self-affirmation, the risk of adventure, my self-respect and the respect of others pointed to the passionate teacher I think I am today. In adolescence, I remember many times when I would liberate my imagination while I was walking alone from school to the train station. I would dream, seeing myself in the classroom teaching the syntax of the Portuguese language. I would daydream.

Awake, I would dream of being a teacher. In my conversations with myself, sometimes on my way from school to the train station, sometimes during the trip from Recife to Jaboatao, alone, or when, during sleepless nights, I would play with the idea of being a teacher. At nineteen years of age the need to help my family economically led me to teaching and to my ever present love for the study of the Portuguese language. There is always a need in our lives that pushes us and makes us do things. My father died when I was thirteen and the financial hardship was always present in spite of all the efforts of my older sister, Stella, and my older brothers, Armando and Temistocles.

I always knew that I had a good command of the mysteries of the Portuguese language and I also knew that I was passionately attracted to linguistic problems. The more I experimented by teaching youths like me, the more I was becoming convinced that I was really becoming a teacher, something that I always wanted to be.

When I turned twenty-two years of age I met my first wife, Elza, whom you met personally. She was a great educator. Very few teachers worked as she did in early childhood education and very few teachers gave themselves so unselfishly and passionately to the task of challenging young children to read and write. She knew how to work with children without having to resort to manipulation, nor did she abandon them in the limitless horizon of a laissez-faire pedagogy. Elza knew very well how to live the tension between freedom and authority. I was a syntax teacher. That's how I met Elza. She had to take a professional test for promotion in her career as a teacher and she sought my help concerning some tutoring in the Portuguese material. Because of this Portuguese syntax class I am today a grandfather of eight grandchildren. We got married a year later and

Elza's influence in my life was enormous. She died, as you know, and I also almost died. The pain from her death profoundly affected me. I almost died as well.

Carlos Torres: She was very strong. . . .

Paulo Freire: She was very strong, very strong, but, at the same time extremely sweet. And the sweetness to which I am referring does not have any negative connotations. It is a necessary ingredient to a true strength. It is like the tenderness of Che Guevara.

Carlos Torres: She knew how to love. . . .

Paulo Freire: Yes, she knew how to love. However, one day, even though engulfed in my pain, I decided to live again. Life presented itself before me as a duty, as a right, and also as a pleasure. To live and love. I discovered something that, for me, is obvious today: the more you are loved and you love, the more you can love. The less you are loved and love, the less you can love. I am in love again. Another woman helped me to return to life to which I have a right and to which I have a duty.

Ana Maria, or simply Nita, as I call her, did not come to me so as to substitute for Elza or to continue Elza's image in the same way I did not come into her life to substitute for her deceased husband, Raul, or to perpetuate his image.

To love again does not mean, nor does it require, that we kill the memories, suffocate the memories, and kill the life that one shared with someone else so as to forget the other person, and negate the past. To love again, as a healthy and legitimate gesture, requires only that one never buries the memories of the loved one with his or her physical death.

Nita did not come to substitute for Elza nor to continue her
legacy. She came, as she told me, in her excellent book,[1] "to
reinvent from the losses, a life with love."

Carlos Torres: She is different. . . .

Paulo Freire: Yes. She is different.

Carlos Torres: She was also your student some time ago?

Paulo Freire: Yes. Nita was my student in high school, a
private high school owned by her father, in Recife. She was
my student in Portuguese. I am twelve years her senior and
she is younger than Elza. There is also something important
in this: that I have been able to restart life again.

This capacity to begin always anew, to make, to reconstruct, and to not spoil, to refuse to bureaucratize the mind,
to understand and to live life as a process—live to become—
is something that always accompanied me throughout life.
This is an indispensable quality of a good teacher: To always
begin—it does not matter if it is to begin again—with the
same force, or with the same energy. I remember with much
joy one morning when I was talking to five different classes
about this same content. If it were not possible for me at
seven A.M. to say something about adjectives and, in the
nine A.M. class to say something totally contrary, it was possible and necessary to move myself in different times with
the same joy, and the same curiosity of someone who learns
from teaching. The teacher has a duty to "relive," to be
"reborn" in each moment of his or her practice so that the

---

1. Freire, Ana Maria Aranjo (1989) *Anal fabetismo no Brasil.* São Paulo: Inep/
Cortex Editora.

content that he or she teaches is alive and not stale motions or what Whitehead calls, "inert ideas."[2]

But, finally, as I began establishing and living relationships with groups of students, as I began teaching them the grammar of Portuguese, I began to become a teacher. And it was through becoming a teacher that, necessarily, I became an educator. There is something, from the perspective of my understanding of the process through which I became an educator, that seems to be fundamentally important. I am referring to the quasi-addiction that overtook me and that I shall never reject: thinking about practice. In the beginning, possibly, I did not really know how to do this. It was as if it were a type of instinct that led me to think, to investigate what I was doing. The more I thought about the practice to which I was committing myself the more I understood what I was doing and, thus, I prepared myself to practice better. This is how I learned always and always to look for the help of theories so I could improve my practice. This is also how I learned to not dichotomize theory and practice, and to never perceive them as being isolated from each other, but in permanent contradictory and dialectical relationship.

To follow up on your question and expand my answer I should talk about another fundamental moment in my development as an educator that has to do, for this very reason, with my preoccupation with educational problems. It is the exact moment that I usually call "my reencounter with rural and urban workers." In my childhood I had had friends with whom I played, soccer friends in the open fields, swimming friends by the river who were the children of the underclass, sons of field and urban workers. I learned a great deal from

2. Whitehead, Alfred N. *The Aims of Education and other Essays.* New York: Free Press, 1967, pp. 1–2.

them and their families about the cruel poverty in the hills
and valleys of Recife.

When I turned twenty-five years of age I was invited to
work in a social service institution that provided services to
urban workers and fishermen. My educational work with
this institution took me to rural as well as poor urban areas
near Recife.[3] If, in my childhood, I lived together with sons
and daughters of peasants and the urban working poor, now,
at twenty-five years of age, through the Social Services Industry, I reestablished my conviviality with fishermen, the
urban working poor, and peasants. It is for this reason that
I speak of a "re-encounter."

This re-encounter, without a doubt, marked, in a rich way,
my life. Perhaps I can today say, without fear of making a
mistake, that the years I spent working almost daily with
peasants, and the working poor of the urban area of Pernambuco, my state, making pedagogical errors and mistakes, but
also learning how to make my practice better, were fundamental years for the development of many of my ideas today.
These years were very important in shaping me as an educator. I would finally say, to conclude my answer to your question, that, without those learning years with the peasants,
the urban working poor, the fishermen who were always part
of my exercise in critical thinking and practice, it would be
almost impossible to have written, years later, *Pedagogy of
the Oppressed*, in Chile, during my exile.

Carlos Torres: Thank you very much, Paulo. Let me pose
to you another question which has emerged from your comments. You were experimenting with yourself, with your

---

3. The institutional reference is to the **Social Service of Industry**, SESI, a private institution created by the National Confederation of Industries in Brazil.

imagination, with your own dreams. You were a very curious child. How is this notion of experience, which is so important in the development of *Pedagogy of the Oppressed*, linked to the notion of systematic, rigorous theorizing in the social sciences and education? Is it possible to start thinking about and of your own experience and then move into the realm of thinking about theory, social theory?

Paulo Freire: It seems so, yes. I would like to underline the excellence of your question, and its epistemological nature. Your question highlights the focus of one of my permanent struggles—that of not allowing myself to be seduced by the temptation of dichotomies in which we lose ourselves, preventing us from ever comprehending the world.

Theory–practice, popular knowledge–scientific knowledge, manual work–intellectual work, culture–nature, consciousness–world, reading the word–reading the world are some of the "undichotomizables" that we usually separate in a formal and mechanical manner. Let's consider dichotomy to which I made reference earlier: theory—practice. For me there is no way to underestimate or overestimate one or the other. There is no way to reduce one to another. One implies the other, in a necessary dialectical and contradictory relationship. In itself, inverse in its refusal of theoretical reflection, practice, in spite of its importance, is not sufficient to offer me a knowledge that explains the raison d'être of relations among objects. Practice does not by itself represent a theory about itself. But, without practice theory runs the risk of wasting time, of diminishing its own validity as well as the possibility of remaking itself. In the final analysis, theory and practice, in their relationships, become mutually necessary as they complement each other. In this sense, there is always built into practice, a certain hidden theory, as there is, in a theoretical project not born from a concrete practice, a future practice that will evaluate the theoretical hypothesis.

The question for me is how to unveil practice in the sense of acquiring knowledge or recognizing in it the theory that is minimally or not yet perceived. Moreover, I would say that the issue is how to discover in practice the rigor with which we approach reality, from the reality within which we act, that would give us each time a more critical knowledge, transcending the pure "knowledge of a ready-made experience." The very task of unveiling a practice, of examining its rigor or its lack of rigor, is a theoretical task, a theoretical practice. For this reason, I spoke a lot at the beginning of our conversation about the quasi-addiction of thinking about practice that I never rejected. The challenge is to think about practice as theoretical task or theoretical practice. It is for this reason that, the more critically and rigorously I think about the practice with which I participate and the practice of others, the more possibility I have, first, to comprehend the raison d'être of the very practice; and second, for the same reason, to expand the capacity to make my practice better. Therefore, to think about my experience as practice inserted in a social practice is serious and indispensable work. What is regrettable, I repeat, is to separate mechanically the world of practice and the world of theory. To think that theoretical practice can only take place in the pure universe of academia dislodged from the concrete reality outside academia is to commit a mistake as fatal as negating the importance of the serious theoretical efforts in academia.

All the time before I wrote *Pedagogy of the Oppressed* and the time during which I wrote it represented moments full of practice about which I thought theoretically. I could never understand the meaning of texts without first having a comprehension of the context of texts. I could never understand the reading of the written word without the reading of the world that pushed me to rewrite the world, that is, its transformation. And when I speak of the world I am not speaking exclusively about the trees and the animals that I love very much, and the mountains and the rivers. I am not speaking exclusively of the nature of which I am a part, but I am speaking also of the social structures, politics, culture, history, of which I am also a part.

Carlos Torres: I appreciate the comment. I understand that the moment of practice and the moment of theory are two different moments, but they ought to be related because in practicing you may be able to unveil the theoretical component of that practice.

Paulo Freire: Yes, yes.

Carlos Torres: And in theorizing about practice you might be able to guide practice better. But, of course you realize and you have said many times, that there are different complexities in both moments. The moment of theory means logical articulation of concepts, time to reflect. It has its own logic. While the moment of practice sometimes calls upon intuition, quick decision making. And of course that in itself poses, for some people, insurmountable obstacles to linking the two of them. And your call is that in reading the text and reading the context you have to find, maybe a methodology, maybe an approach, by which you can do both as well.

Paulo Freire: I would not like to give you the impression that I am being simplistic in my treatment of a theme as complex and serious as this. The necessary relations between text and context, word and world, being already of a theoretical nature, require a practice that is coherent. But this is not sufficient to resolve the impasse to which you refer. It is important that I have such understanding, but it is also fundamental, indispensable, that I develop conceptually so I can live it or practice it. In the final analysis, it is the same as requiring that we think about practice. The practice of thinking about practice deprived of a serious and well-founded theoretical tool would result in a sterile and boring game. Many meetings about the evaluation of practice conducted by militant groups that work in poor areas end up being watered down and eventually die out for this very reason. I am now reminded of an experience I had, years back, with a committed youth group that was working with literacy in poor areas of São Paulo. I was invited by the youth group to visit. The group wanted to discuss with me "some of the obstacles they were encountering in their work." The central problem they had was the lack of interest of the majority of the educators who were part of the community-based literacy groups. I asked them if they met systematically to evaluate what they were doing. "Yes," they said, "but, for about two months their meetings had become tiresome and no longer provided the satisfaction they once had. For about two months," they continued, "we haven't made any headway in these meetings. The problems are always the same and we never speak about solutions, about strategies. We can never point to the possible reasons for the difficulties."

What was taking place was, up to a certain point, that the group leadership did not have sufficient theoretical knowledge to, in the process of thinking about the practice of the people involved, unveil with them the obstacles and their raison d'être. All of a sudden, the leadership began to feel lost. In reality, the leadership lacked the theoretical tools to help it illuminate the practice about which the militants were attempting to think, but were unable to do so. In fact, it is not possible to work with literacy, no matter whether it is carried out with children, adolescents, or adults, without a minimum of theoretical intimacy with Piaget, Vygotsky, Luria, Emilia Ferreiro, Madalena Freire Wefford, Ana Teberosky, Constance Kamii, Esther Gnossi, Magda Soares, to mention only a few. Or without a minimum of intimacy with the practice as well as theory of Vera Barreto and Fatima Freire Dowbor.

Perhaps it would be of interest to point out once more the relationship between theory and practice, to call attention to the fact that it is not possible to have practice without programming permanent evaluation into the process of practice. To practice always implies the evaluation of practice. And the practice of programming that extends from the process of the evaluation of practice is a theoretical practice.

All those years I spent working with the fishermen, the rural and urban working poor around Pernambuco, were years of capital importance to what I would do many years later. These years were not only about doing but about doing what, that is, they were years of praxis, of theory and practice, of action and of reflection, of programming and evaluation.

You made reference in your last comment about intuition. I would like to insist on one point. For me it is impossible to know rigorously while depreciating intuition, feelings, dreams, and desires. It is my entire body that, socially, knows. I cannot, in the name of exactness and rigor, negate my body, my emotions, and my feelings. I know very well that to know is not to guess but to know also passes through a guessing process. What I do not have any right to do, if I am rigorous, serious, is to remain satisfied with my intuition. I should submit the object of my intuition to the rigorous tests it desires, but never depreciate its role in coming to knowledge. For me, intuition is a necessary initial component to critical thinking.

There is an issue that involves the question of practice and theory, of practice and its programming and evaluation to which I would like also to address. It deals with the ease with which specialists who had nothing to do with the development of a certain practice, in the fields of social science, are sometimes called to evaluate such practice. The notion that feelings corrupt research and its findings, the fear of intuition, the categorical negation of emotion and passion, the belief in technicisms—all of this ends up convincing many that, the more neutral we are in our actions, the more objective and efficient we will be. We become, therefore, more exact, more scientific, and not ideological or journalistic.

I do not want to deny the possibility that a specialist outside the context where the practice took place or is taking place can participate in an evaluation team with positive results. The specialists' effectiveness, however, will depend on their capacity to open up to the soul of the culture where the experience took place or is taking place. It can never be solely dependent upon the specialist's ability to learn about the rationality of the experience through multiple means. To open up to the culture's soul is to allow one to become wet, to become soaked in the cultural and historical waters of those individuals who are involved in the experience.

Carlos Torres: Your metaphorical expression "to become wet, to become soaked in the cultural and historical waters" is very insightful. To become wet to such an extent implies plunging into the world of feelings and, at the same time, attempting a theoretical comprehension of the practice that is taking place. On the other hand, Paulo, I think it's of tremendous importance what you have just said about linking intuition with rigorous knowledge or reasoning, because the more you link the two of them the more your intuition becomes educated, becomes more logically articulated in looking, understanding, and observing reality and coming to conclusions. While the more you link that process of intuition to your logical reasoning, the more your logical reasoning becomes intuitive. And in this kind of opposition, apparent opposition, between the two terms, you become more unified in one way of understanding, comprehending, reality, which includes not only the moment of reasoning, but the empathetic moment of understanding, of feeling with the rest of the people, with those who you are trying to understand, which is very important in education, of course.

Let me now ask you about a word that you have used for more than thirty years already—though you stopped using it a few years ago—the notion of *conscientização,* that very difficult neologism in English that some people have translated as "critical consciousness," or "awareness." What does it mean for you, the notion of conscientization and why did you stop using it some years ago?

Paulo Freire: I believe I can begin by saying that one of the qualities that we develop in in the process of becoming social beings aware of our history, in becoming animal-people— women and men—was the capacity to observe curiously, inquiringly, the world around us, contemplating it, frightening us, as if we were preparing ourselves so later on we would become filled with wonder before the world. In this way we would then act on the world and perceive things while acting, while observing, while contemplating. We learn things about the world by acting and changing the world around us. It is to this process of change, of transforming the material world from which we emerged, of which the creation of the cultural and historical world takes place. This transformation of the world was done by us while it makes and remakes us, which I have been calling "writing" the world even before we say the word and long before we write it.

Jim and Andra, my dear German shepherds, also observe and see the trees in the backyard of our house in whose shadow they take refuge from the hot afternoons in São Paulo. Possibly, Jim and Andra do not go beyond seeing the trees. They could not, for example, establish any relationship among the fruits produced by the trees and the birds that, in certain periods of the year, take delight in them and delight us with their songs and their clamor.

Jim and Andra will not perceive the color changes of leaves as a sign of seasonal change. The seasons for them remain at the level of the sensibility toward hot or cold, but they do not have a name to refer to the seasons of the year. Jim and Andra do not speak about these relations. I do not only look and see a tree but I have also the memory of other trees that I can distinguish from those that I see. I do not only speak about trees but I also have the concept tree.

Exactly because we have become human beings, doers of things, transformers, contemplators, speakers, social beings, we necessarily end up as producers of knowledge. As a necessity we search for beauty and morality. In the process of producing and acquiring knowledge, we end up also by learning to "take distance" from objects, a contradictory way of approaching them. The establishment of distance from objects presupposes the perception of them in their relations with other objects. The establishment of distance from objects implies coming to consciousness about them, but this does not signify yet that I may be interested or that I may feel capable of going beyond the pure verification of objects to apprehend the raison d'etre of these objects. It is in this sense that coming to consciousness, being a human form of being in the world, is not yet conscientization as I understand it.

Conscientization[4] is the deepening of the coming of consciousness. There can be no conscientization without coming first to consciousness, but not all coming to consciousness extends necessarily into conscientization. It is in this sense that the pure coming to consciousness that lacks a cautious curiosity, critical reflection, the rigorousness of procedures of approximation to objects remains at the level of common sense.

Conscientization, for this very reason, cannot take place in a practice that lacks the indispensable seriousness of wanting to know rigorously. But, those who want to know rigorously know also that the process of knowing is neither neutral nor indifferent. To work, therefore, in a conscientizing posture, whether with Brazilian peasants, Spanish-Americans or Africans, or with university people from any part of the world, is to search with rigor, with humility, without the arrogance of the sectarians who are overly certain about their universal certainties, to unveil the truths hidden by ideologies that are more alive when it is said that they are dead.

Perhaps it is important to run the risk of reiterating. The conscientizing effort refuses, on the one hand, the elitist devaluation with which sometimes, even some progressive intellectuals treat the knowledge of lived experience—popular cultural knowledge. On the other hand, by respecting this knowledge, the conscientizing effort refuses to be immobilized by the knowledge of lived experience. In other words, to remain at the level of popular cultural knowledge,

---

4. On this issue, see "Avertisement" in L'Education, Pratique de la Liberté (1975). Paris: Les Editions de Cerf.

in peace, as if this knowledge were sufficient is inappropriate. On the contrary, I insist that lived experience be used as a point of departure so as to transcend it. Moreover, the true conscientizing practice, precisely because it does not dichotomize the reading of the text from the reading of the context to which it refers or to which one intends to apply the text, never accepts being reduced to a simple "militant" discourse—empty, authoritarian, and ineffective. Because it is more than the exclusive coming to consciousness of reality, conscientization requires a rigorous comprehension of itself. For this very reason, it is not possible to have a real conscientization in neutral teaching, "sterilized" from content. Isn't it a pity that the educator, in order not to commit a "sin" against the "pure nature" of schools, fails to tell the student that grammar, by itself, is not sufficient to explicate the agreement rule in Portuguese since even when you have one thousand women in the room with only one man, agreement is achieved with the masculine form.

You inquired about my having stopped making direct reference to the word *conscientization*. It is true. The last time that I expanded on this topic was in 1974—it had already been four years, more or less, since I had stopped using it. I last used it in the World Council of Churches in Geneva, with Ivan Illich. It was there that Ivan Illich once again used the concept of "deschooling" and I again used conscientization. Naturally, however, in not using the word for a time, I did not refute its signification. As an educator, therefore as a political person, I was always involved with the most profound comprehension of this concept in my theoretical and practical activities.

I had, without a doubt, reasons to stop using the word conscientization. During the seventies, with exception, of course, people would speak or write about conscientization as if it were a magical pill to be applied in different doses with an eye toward changing the world. One thousand pills for a reactionary boss. Ten pills for an authoritarian union leader. Fifty pills for intellectuals whose practice contradicted their discourse, and so forth.

It seemed to me then, and I spoke to Elza about this issue, that, on the one hand, I should stop using the term conscientization and, on the other hand, try to better clarify, in interviews, seminars, and articles—what in fact I did— what I intended to say of the conscientizing process. Thus diminishing the risks of an idealistic interpretation. That is just as woeful as the positivistic and mechanicist position.

I hope I have answered your question.

Carlos Torres: It does, it does. Now, what's the relationship in your mind, in your conceptualization, not only in terms of conscientization as a term, but in terms of the practice of conscientization in literacy training? How could you link literacy training, which for some people is conceived as merely teaching how to read, write, and do basic literacy with the notion of conscientization or the project of conscientization?

Paulo Freire: Your question leaves me intellectually unquiet, excited, and it is almost impossible to contain myself. I will try, however, to be succinct in my response. Look, Carlos, one of the tasks that we have as teachers in our daily activities—it does not matter with whom we work, if it is with children, adolescents, university students, peasants, or the urban poor, in literacy or postliteracy is the following: If in reality education is also—not exclusively—a certain theory of knowledge put into practice, this means that it is impossible to think about education without thinking about knowledge. In other words it is impossible to think about the transference of knowledge without thinking about knowledge itself.

I am certain that the educational practice is always this, if not only this. One of our tasks when we teach, for example, when you teach at UCLA,[5] beyond teaching sociology, in my point of view, is teaching how to know. You should teach how to think correctly, which is not done through the teaching of content, it is true. If teaching and learning are part of the same process of knowing, the moment you teach sociology you should also make it clear to your students how you study, how you approach the object of knowledge, what is the meaning for you of the search for knowledge. Sadly, in most cases, we consider this to be the hidden aspect of our private or intellectual life and we lose ourselves in long expositions about the object. Worse yet, almost always we make immense speeches profiling the knowledge itself. Let's return now to the relationship between the literacy teachers and their adult students.

I am convinced that during a great part of the initial activities in which literacy teachers and students are involved the subject revolves around the following: the literacy teacher who teaches the word and its implications with the world; the literacy students who learn about writing and reading; in the end, both find themselves, through the mutual commitment to teach and learn, engaged in a common process of knowing. They are both knowing subjects, each on his or her level.

The first phase, from the point of view of a theory of knowledge according to which the student cannot be reduced to an empty vessel, I make reference to in *Pedagogy of the Oppressed*. At the same time the educator deals with

5. University of California at Los Angeles.

the teaching of the word taken from a phrase, he or she must also be alert with regard to the findings of Emilia Ferreiro, or Madalena Freire Wefford (before them Piaget, Vygotsky, Luria to only cite a few). I propose, above all, supporting the curious and critical position that requires "establishing distance" from the object so that contradictorily by approaching it, we come to know it.

In this sense, literacy in its profound sense is not only, nor can it rigorously be, the moment in that mechanically the bureaucratic mind of the educator initiates the bureaucratic "treatment" of the student's mind, filling it with phrases, words, syllables, letters, and exclamations!

Literacy as acquisition, production, and reinvention of the written language and necessarily read should, for the sake of its seriousness, constitute itself during the time of the introduction of how to think. By respecting the common-sense knowledge to begin to bring the students closer to a more profound comprehension of language, of the raison d'être of things, of their difficulties, so as to transcend them.

Let's return a little to the question of "establishing distance." Suppose I show a photograph of an area of São Paulo to a group of literacy students pointing not only to the concrete poverty of the area but also to the human misery. This picture represents a portion of São Paulo, reflecting the reality of a large number of literacy students in the city. By showing the photograph (codification) I invite or challenge them to "establish distance" from the totality. In the final analysis I attempt to challenge them to see a part of São Paulo, their São Paulo, the one where they live, suffer, endure pain, dream, and die. This constitutes an exercise of knowing.

A great Latin American educator from Equador, Rosa Maria Torres, used codification in the process of teaching literacy as I did for the same epistemological reasons. She preferred a pedagogical path that could be classified as postmodern: she used codifications that depicted contexts of happiness, joy, and satisfaction. By discussing with students the things that they lacked, she engaged them in a discussion about their rights which enabled her to attain great success. Rosa Maria Torres' approach was, perhaps, more efficient than mine.

Only ignorance that may be everything but saintly, could attempt to reduce the relationship between language and literacy to banal bas, bes, bis, bos, bus.

Carlos Torres: I would like to ask Professor Paulo Freire to offer to those who will be in the conference of literacy in Edmonton during the second week of October 1990 what you expect to accomplish.

Paulo Freire: In reality, I never, or almost never, feel comfortable doing what you are asking me to do right now. I will attempt, in a few words, to say something as if I were there.

In the first place to teach someone to read and write is something that is very serious and demands of those who teach a high level of respect for those who are learning to read and write. What do I mean by a serious respect for the literacy learners? I am referring to the respect for the knowledge that the learners always bring to the classroom. It does not matter if this knowledge is generated from their daily lived experience, common sense—what the learners bring is their own body that is sometimes tired and beaten, and their body's memory. I refer to the respect for the students' language, their accent, their syntax, and their semantics. I also refer to a respect for their culture, and above all, for their cultural identity, which is also class specific.

It is necessary, on the one hand, to make it very clear that the principal question regarding literacy, the teaching of reading and writing, is not of a technical nature. The principal questions of literacy are always of a political, ideological, and scientific nature to which we add technical issues as well. The point of departure is the decision, the political will to conduct literacy, the identification of resources, and the rigorous preparation of teachers.

There is also something which, even though enmeshed in the political nature of literacy I referred to earlier, I never disassociate from my comprehension of the educational struggle in general, and, literacy, in particular. I am referring to the utopian dream that always served as the impetus for all my political and pedagogical adventures. My utopian dream has to do with a society that is less unjust, less cruel, more democratic, less discriminatory, less racist, less sexist. To teach to read and to write should not ever be reduced to the reductionistic, inexpressive, insipid task that serves to silence the voices of struggle that try to justify our presence in the world and not our blind accommodation to an unjust and discriminatory world. To teach to read and write is not a pastime for us and not a favor nor a charity that we practice. Teaching literacy is, above all, a social and political commitment.

Carlos Torres: Well, thank you very much, on behalf of all those who will be participating in the Edmonton conference. Thank you for your message. I hope we accomplish what you ask us to do.

Let's now discuss your experiences as a public figure in the field of pedagogy. Over the years you have been criticized on a number of levels. You were criticized for your apolitical views of education. You were criticized for a naive perception of democracy in Brazil. You were criticized because you were considered a pedagogic populist, someone who'll go to the masses, to the grassroots, to give to the masses whatever they request without forcing the people to move to a higher stage of understanding of reality. And finally you were criticized because some people understood you as saying that education is not directive. So you were criticized for being nondirective, and in being nondirective, your message will be that education is not a rigorous act of transmission of knowledge. And therefore if that notion of a rigorous act of transmission of knowledge is abandoned, then the whole process of training teachers will be undermined. What would you say to us, now, maybe ten, fifteen, twenty years after being criticized in this manner?

Paulo Freire: Before attempting to answer any question regarding the critique of my work, which has, in a general manner, been discussed in different texts that I have published, perhaps it would be interesting to point out that generally I do not go to the field for this type of fight. I prefer dialogue over polemics, which is a type of fight that leads to nowhere.

Let's begin with the last criticism that raises the question of directivity or nondirectivity in education. I am going to forget for now that six years ago I discussed this issue extensively in a book published in São Paulo.[6]

How can I negate the directivity of education as directivity is, itself, part and parcel of the nature of education? Education constantly marches beyond itself. There is no education without objectives, without ends. It is precisely this that by making it directive, one prevents its neutrality or the neutrality of the educator. Beginning with the fact that all educa-

---

6. See Freire, Paulo and Guimaraes, Sergio, 2 volumes. Rio, Paz e Terra, 1983.

tional practice is directive by its very nature, the question that coherent progressive educators must deal with is what do they need to do to diminish the distance between what they say and what they do so as not to allow directivity to turn into authoritarianism or manipulation. By the same token, in avoiding directivity they need to prevent losing themselves in the lack of clear limits that often leads into a laissez-faire approach. I have never defended either of these positions. Thus, I do not accept false criticism.

Another point that is for me very important concerning the criticism about my lack of directivity is the question of knowledge and the transmission of knowledge. How can I neglect to provide direction that is, I repeat, part and parcel of education itself. To refuse to give direction is tantamount to rejecting education as a rigorous transmission of knowledge.

What I reject is not the directivity of education. What I reject is how knowledge is transferred or transmitted from one subject to another that, in this case, would passively receive the "gift" given to him or her. Knowledge is socially created, invented, and reinvented and is learned. Knowledge is produced. A student knows, to the degree that he or she develops a profound comprehension of the content taught, that he or she has learned it. In order to learn one has to truly comprehend content. Because I apprehend that I learn and, by apprehending in this fashion, I know. I do not know by the pure oral or graphic transference of a concept's profile. Let's continue with these criticisms. In the first place it is important that they are made particularly when the criticisms are honest, competent, and serious.

What appears to me to be incorrect is a person who criticizes an author's work, selectively leaving out eight or more of his or her books and, without alerting the readers, gives the impression that he or she is criticizing the complete works of the author. And what is worse is that the author is still living. I do not consider this type of criticism to be serious and honest.

It is true that in my first book[7]—and I myself have critiqued this work in other books that I published in the beginning of the seventies—I do not make any reference to the political nature of education. But this is not the case with my other works beginning with *Pedagogy of the Oppressed*. I do not believe that this type of criticism has any validity today.

The last criticism to which you refer—that I am a populist educator—does not say anything to me. At any rate, I discussed this issue extensively in two books published in Brazil and the United States. I am referring to *Learning to Question* with Antonio Faundez, and *Literacy: Reading the Word and the World* with Donaldo Macedo.

Carlos Torres: Paulo, I am quite impressed with your answer. So what you are claiming is that a democratic teacher is neither authoritarian nor a laissez-faire. Now, in promoting this democratic substantiveness or substantivity as you said, we have to be aware of the distinction between hidden curriculum and the explicit curriculum. There is no doubt in my mind that you argue for an explicit curriculum with a particular kind of content with a particular methodology and the like. What about the hidden curriculum? What about the social relationships established at the level of the classroom? What about the values promoted in the sometimes unspoken relationships between teacher and student?

Paulo Freire: Perhaps we have reached now in our conversation one of its important moments. Not only thinking in terms of the Brazilian but also with respect to the interna-

---

7. *A Proposito de uma Administraçao*. Reife: Emprensa Universitaria, 1961.

tional context. In order to address or question its content, I feel obliged to rethink an issue that I have spoken intensively about in seminars both in and outside of Brazil. I am referring to what I call virtues or qualities of a progressive educator. These qualities or virtues are, in the final analysis, created by us in our practice. It is not easy to participate in a permanent struggle against preconceived notions that are ingrained in our bodies, expecting our body to move in accordance to these preconceptions.

One of these indispensable virtues of a progressive educator has to do with the coherence between discourse and practice. To diminish the distance between these then represents an exercise that we should require of ourselves. It is one thing to speak and write about democratic and creative relations between teacher and students, it is another to repress the students because they ask the teacher uncomfortable questions. It is one thing to speak of teachers' seriousness, the academic rigorousness, the necessary ethics, the other is to include in the bibliography books recently published but which the teachers themselves haven't read.

Let us now think about the hidden curriculum. I believe that the first approximation to this concept so as to denude it will reveal to us that in its intimacy we will find a large number of preconceptions. On the other hand, these preconceptions obfuscate the reality within which we work and about which we speak. On the other hand, they make us become myopic, which creates difficulty in seeing the reality for what it is. It is for this reason that the hidden curriculum is sometimes more powerful in its execution than an overt one.

A teacher, for example, can be theoretically clear concerning his or her duty of respecting his or her students, their cultural identity, but the power of the authoritarian ideology with which he or she has been previously inculcated ends up winning, forcing him or her to contradict the theoretical discourse. And, he or she is left with very little choice but to make an appeal to escapism so as to justify his or her authoritarianism that, in the Brazilian case, is deep-rooted in the sociocultural traditions of our society. Even the content, especially the way in which it is taught, its mystification, its magical power to "save" the subordinate classes, all of this that appears half explicit and half hidden has a great deal to do with the critical comprehension of the hidden curriculum.

Hence, I am convinced that one of the most important central tasks in the preparation of teachers is to invite them to think critically about what they do in their practice. To think about practice is something I have insistently proposed throughout the years. The most hidden aspects of the hidden curriculum are found, permit me to reiterate, in the social, historical, cultural, and class-based experiences of the society of which teachers are a part. Thus, for this very reason, we pay very little attention in the historical development of our society.

I believe that I am being obvious when, in referring to the hidden curriculum, I am treating it with the same amplitude as the overt curriculum. In this way we are prevented from reducing our comprehension of the overt curriculum to a mere relation of programmatic content. In reality, an understanding of the curriculum involves the entire life of schools, what is done or not done in them and the relations among all of those individuals that make up schools. It involves the force of the ideology and its representation not only in terms of ideas but also as concrete practice. In the hidden curriculum, the discourse about the body, the facial features, are more powerful than the oral discourse. The concrete authoritarian practice asphyxiates the democratic discourse pure and simple.

A very useful tool that may help us in the archaeology of discovering what lies hidden in school corridors, school yards, classrooms, lunch time, in short all that happens in school is video. Video helps us capture many of our spontaneous reactions, many exclamations with respect to a contradictory discourse that was recently spoken. Through video we can see ourselves in our classroom simply walking through the corridors, or the way we talk to students so as to help us analyze and critique our own behavior in school. It would help us understand better our own practice and to perceive the gulf that almost always exists between what we say and what we do. Naturally, it will be able to confront ideology exclusively through discussion. Therefore, I am convinced that the more we think and analyze the ideological power the better equipped we will be to struggle against it so as to experiment with new educational practice.

It is exactly along these lines that progressive educators who have been touched by the democratic dream, discuss with children, their students, about how difficult it is to construct and achieve true democracy, but always to stress the importance and the beauty of democracy. Once in a while, teachers should call students' attention to a small conflict that led to an outburst or explosion resulting in an antidemocratic behavior. They should ask: "Why did I allow myself to become lost in this way?"

Finally, I believe that Brazilian society is presently participating in a historical climate that is highly favorable to democratic experiences. Maybe we have enjoyed our present democratic freedom so much that we are passionately dreaming about it. However, this taste and this passion for freedom coexist with authoritarian traditions and practices, resulting in one of our ambiguities.

Carlos Torres: Well, I am really very impressed with the

answer, and I have to challenge you once more. I think, when you were talking about democracy, the notion of democratic teacher arose. What sort of teacher is this? In this context, I remember a statement made by an important populist figure in Latin America, Juan Domingo Peron, of Argentina. Peron always wanted to have functionaries in public service who were at the same time honest, intelligent, and Peronist. He complained that those who were Peronist were neither honest or intelligent. This was a quite puzzling situation and resulted in his inability to find the perfect functionary for his own government.

Now, what kind of teacher are we talking about? You mentioned that this should be someone who is politically clean, who is competent technically, someone who has a thirst for knowledge, someone who is always becoming. And, of course, if you agree to be always becoming, you must have a tremendous sense of confidence in that process of becoming knowing that you have started somewhere and you are going somewhere. That sense of confidence may lead you to resort to authoritarianism as a way to prove your authority as a teacher. Or it may lead you to a laissez-faire approach as a way of saying "I'm giving up, I will simply go with the flow."

Now, some people have complained to me, sometimes, that Paulo Freire is such a gifted teacher, such a brilliant facilitator, he's asking all to be like him. He's asking everyone to have the same confidence in becoming, to have the same thirst for knowledge, to be as competent politically as he is, to be as competent technically as he is. What would you say to those who complain that these sorts of teachers do not exist, and that we had better work with whatever we have at hand?

Paulo Freire: In the first place, I would like to say, with false modesty (which it seems to me to be more reproachable than the declared lack of modesty), that I do not consider myself a privileged teacher but, as I have said throughout our conversation, a passionate teacher.

In reality, once in a while I come across this type of criticism. It appears obvious to me that only this type of teacher, but any type of teacher, does not appear by accident, but through the interplay between social, economic, political and cultural forces among which one finds the political will to prepare serious and competent teachers.

I think that a good way to answer your question is to ask another question: Will it be easy to train really good social scientists: Good physicists? Good medical doctors? Good mathematicians? Good engineers? Good agronomists? The answer is no. It is not easy. The fundamental question for me is if it is possible or not; if the dream is possible or not. If it is possible, we need to know if it is for now or tomorrow. The rest, the question concerning possible dreams of today is a permanent question. This question is followed by another inquiry. How can we make possible today the dream that appears to be of and for tomorrow. In truth, one of our political tasks that we need to assume is to make viable the dreams that appear impossible. In other words, we need to diminish the distance between the dream and its materialization.

You, I, and countless numbers of educators know that education is not the key to the transformation of the world, but we also know that the transformation of the world is an educational task in itself. We know that education cannot accomplish all, but it can achieve some things. Its power resides precisely in its weakness. It behooves us to put the power of education at the service of our dreams. I do not have any doubt that one of the tasks that education can accomplish is to make our democratic process more consistent.

If we believe in this possibility whose materialization passes through a struggle without truces in favor of a serious, competent, politically lucid, joyful public school system, it becomes also imperative to fight for our dreams, and to make it possible to create, and to count on committed and progressive teachers about whom we have been talking.

So people do not think that I am digressing, I should say that I know that this struggle is a fight for power. Perhaps, to be more exact, it is a fight for the reinvention of power. The reinvention of power is also a possible dream. If you pretend to become engaged in the fight for this dream, you have to begin some day.

I would also like to add a few more reflections that have to do with democratic teachers and their dreams. For me, Carlos, it is absolutely impossible to democratize our schools without transcending the preconceptions against the lower and subordinate classes, against the children who are called "poor," without transcending our preconceptions against their language, their culture, and the preconceptions against the knowledge that these children bring to school. It is impossible to democratize schools without really opening them to the real participation of parents and the community in determining the schools' destiny. To participate means much more than to "offer" on some weekends to parents the opportunity to repair schools, which is, in fact, the responsibility of the state. We never hear of this type of parent participation—fixing and cleaning schools—in the well-to-do neighborhood of São Paulo.

To participate is to discuss, to have voice, acquiring it through the educational politics of schools and the reorganization of their budgets. Finally, Carlos, without believing the dream, without betting on it, it is impossible to realize the dream.

Carlos Torres: I very much appreciate that comment, Paulo. Let me try to conclude with this section of criticisms of your work by focusing in on a couple of issues, essentially in an effort to relate to one of your major themes. One of the criticisms is that after you wrote *Pedagogy of the Oppressed,* twenty years ago, you stopped systematizing your own ideas. You stopped working systematically toward enhancing the standard, the pedagogical, political, sociological, philosophical understanding that permeates *Pedagogy of the Oppressed.* Another criticism is that most of your work has been oriented toward understanding education in the national context, but with the growing universalization of capitalization as a world system, to what extent does it make any sense to think of local autonomy, of national autonomy when you have a just national capitalism pervading most of the social, mental, political, ethical, moral structures of Latin America, for example? How could you relate these criticisms to your notion of the political nature of education?

Paulo Freire: Let us consider the first aspect of your question. I think I can say with humility that writers, thinkers, those who say or write about something always have something to say with, at least, an appearance of novelty. But I also believe that it is not only legitimate, but also necessary to say again so as to say what has been said and not always written with clarity in the initial writings.

After I wrote *Pedagogy of the Oppressed* I have not only— from my own point of view—resaid things written in that book in search of a greater clarity of thinking about them, but I have also advanced in my critical comprehension of educational practice. I have done this in interviews, in articles, in some books that I call "dialogical books" where I have established rich dialogues with other intellectuals, and not only Brazilians.

Perhaps, some of these critics have not had the opportunity to read my other books while requiring of me what I cannot give them. I am, in reality, a common man. Nothing more. There is something more that I would like to say to those who criticize me in this manner: Let us suppose that I realize tomorrow that I have really exhausted my capacity to think critically and to produce and write. Will I be happy about this? No. But I will not commit suicide. I will continue to be alive, very alive.

Let us consider the second aspect of the question. Naturally, as an educator, I should be close to the problem posed to me. In many aspects, however, the problem escapes me as a pedagogue, and also you as a social scientist. What we can do with respect to the issue is to call attention to those who read us, who hear us, and work with us about the relations between different levels of action, that is, local, regional, or international. Each one of those that are apparently smaller will have undeniable importance vis-à-vis the global. In the end this has to do with the question of totality and partiality that constitute the action in contradictory relations between one another. Undeniably, the mistake does not rest in considering the partialities. The mistake does not rest in the search for the comprehension of what takes place locally, regionally, or nationally, but in falling into what I call a focalist view of reality in which we look at the comprehension of its totality. By the mere fact of making evident the internationalization of the economy does not put to rest the need to understand what takes place here and now, at the regional and national levels even in view of its interdependency with what is taking place internationally.

The question of the politics of education does not depend on the internationalization of the economy. The politics of education is part and parcel of the very nature of education. Education is just as political here and today as it is in the United States of American there and today. It is just as political in Asia as it is in Europe. It does not matter where or when it has taken place, whether it is more or less complex, education has always been a political act.

Carlos Torres: Professor Paulo Freire, Secretary of Education Paulo Freire, fourteen months after your administration began, what are the joys, what are the sorrows of being not only a political man, but a man in a political position? In such a position you are not only Freire writing about power, but Freire in power.

Paulo Freire: Carlos, this is a beautiful and important question. I have no doubt that I have a great deal to say about the core of your question. I have, in reality, spoken and written a great deal about this issue in Brazilian and foreign journals, newspapers, on radio and television during the past fourteen years.

I would begin by saying that when I was invited by the newly elected mayor of São Paulo, Luiza Erundina, to become part of her government, I was overtaken by doubts, fear, joy, a sense of duty, hope, dreams, and my need for taking risks. I felt the need to be coherent with all I had up to now spoken and written about in education. I also felt the tremendous trust of my party, the Workers' Party admiration and respect for Erundina, for her seriousness as a politician and as a human being, for her competence, and her honesty.

It was not possible for me to say no. But, in spite of my experience in exile that enabled me to participate in the reconstruction of societies that were born from people's liberation struggles, I was surprised to learn how difficult it was to change something. It was difficult but possible. This is evident in the collaborative work I have been doing with colleagues who are part of our working group. It has been difficult because of the ideological, bureaucratic, political, and economic nature that results in dispiritness making people become hopeless servants of the very entrenched administration that always made a lot of promises but never fulfilled any. As I said, the task was difficult but not impossible. Thus, you have a movement that oscillates between suffering, pain, joy, and hope. There is not a day in our administration that we did not experience this oscillation. In the end, we were all involved in a struggle to change what I often refer to as the "face" of schools. Our goal is to make schools not only public but also popular and democratic.

It is natural, therefore, that we suffer in our day-to-day work moments of joy as well as instances of pain. Even today, when I left my office to come and tape this interview with you, one of my assistants came in and told me: "I have good news; we almost finished the most urgent repair of the schools that were gravely in disrepair." In fact, when we took over the Department of Education, we found that 60 percent of the six hundred and fifty-seven schools were in dire need of repair. A great majority needed renovation in all their sections and some of them needed to be almost reconstructed anew. At the same time, however, we found many schools under construction but not finished, some of them a long way from being finished. Nonetheless these schools were adorned with inauguration plaques dated September 1988, two months before the city wide mayoral election in São Paulo. Up to the end of our administration, the school system will have had all the day-to-day problems found in all households: a leaky faucet, an unexpected electrical failure, and a refrigerator that has stopped working.

On the other hand, the political decision to change the face of schools did not hesitate to put into practice the plan to remake the schools, to close the incredible deficits of school desks, among which fifteen thousand were badly broken and thrown in the school yards as if they were being readied for a bonfire. We simultaneously tackled both deficits—the deficit of quantity that took place in the initial chapter of the physical restoration of the city schools, and the quality deficit. Probably, at the same time, these problems do not lend themselves to dichotomies. And as you know, we cannot tackle the problems in education—the increase in teachers' salaries, for example, without thinking first about a permanent teacher education. Unfortunately, due to the limitations of time, we cannot elaborate on this important topic today.

With respect to the changing of the face of schools, for the democratization of schools, I would like to mention another important point that is linked to Senator Mario Covas. A few days before his term expired, he created the so-called school councils that, obviously he could not put into practice. Precisely because of the democratic implications of these councils, they can make viable, as deliberative councils, the participation of parents, students, the school community and alter the local community. The administration of Janio Quadros, that replaced that of Mr. Covas, had preceded us. Quadros's administration simply filed the school councils' initiative away. One of the first acts of Mayor Erundina's administration was to give life to the school councils that we have now begun to implement through serious work in order to clarify their role and importance.

When we consider that our traditions are authoritarian, it was to be expected that some of the schools' principals, whose authority was celebrated, would try to asphyxiate the councils in their birth. In other cases, on the contrary, the newly formed councils exacerbated their power and tried to overshadow the principals. In cases that appear to be in the minority, some councils were learning how to deal with the necessary tensions among them. Learning from the tension helped everyone in the creation of a new understanding of democracy within the schools. This is what happened in practice. Today, there is thinking about the creation of "federations" that would bring together the school councils from various regions or zones, or school districts that divide us administratively.

I do not have any doubt about the need that we have, let me repeat, to insist, whenever possible, to create a practice of a democratic nature—a practice in which we learn how to deal with the tension between authority and freedom, a tension that cannot be avoided unless through the sacrifice of democracy. We have to transcend our ambiguity vis-à-vis the tensions between authority and freedom. The more authentically I live this tension, the less I fear freedom and the less I reject the necessary authority.

These ambiguities give rise to the following well-known positions: it gives rise to practice ungrounded in theory on the one hand and, on the other hand, it produces the elitist theoretic position to which I have already made some references.

I would like to make it very clear that, in my view, to choose theory over practice, for example, implies the dismissal of practice. In contrast, to choose in favor of popular knowledge or community based knowledge negates the importance of theory. The same is true in the choice in favor of authority or freedom. Any of these choices works definitively against democracy.

The community-based camp can be as authoritarian as the elitist perspective. The elitism of the dominant classes is just as reactionary as the elitism of some so-called progressive leaders. To be with the community, to work with the community, does not necessitate the construction of the community as the proprietor of truth and virtue. To be and work with the community means to respect its members, learn from them so one can teach them as well.

Carlos Torres: Let's continue discussing this issue. What you are saying, it seems to me, is that on the one hand there is an ideology of process more than content, more the notion of participation and representation as a set of methods of democratic work, more than as the content of democracy, the democratic work of democracy. Is it possible to argue that one of the problems with this ideology, besides the way it's been generated and the way it's been pervading politics in Latin America, is that it tried to break the dialectical tension between popular knowledge, commonsense, and high culture, the notion of an academic, refined culture representing the best of civilization? With this in mind, what can be done now?

Paulo Freire: I agree with what is implicit in your investigation. The community-based program sectarianism leads to a loss of the more dynamic and contradictory vision of reality. The myopic excess of certainty concerning practice makes the sectarian community-based program undeniably authoritarian. It distorts its democratic intention. The mistake with the sectarian community-based program does not lie in the valorization of the people of the community, but in making them the only repositories of truth and virtue. The mistake does not lie in the criticism, negation, or rejection of academic intellectuals who are arrogant theorists, but in rejecting theory itself, the need for rigor and intellectual seriousness.

It is for this reason that the critical comprehension of community-based programs requires the intelligence of relations between practice and theory, something that I have already spoken a great deal about. One of the political-pedagogical acts that truly progressive educators and community-based movements need to accomplish is the demonstration that theory cannot be separated from practice. Theory is indispensable to the transformation of the world. In truth, there is no practice that does not have a built-in theory. And the more I know the raison d'être not only of the process with which I am involved in changing the society, but also of knowing better the raison d'être of the possible reactions to this challenge, then the more efficaciously I am able to confront the transformative process, and the better I will be able to work towards change.

In reality, without theory we lose ourselves in the middle of the road. But, on the other hand, without practice, we lose ourselves in the air. It is only through the contradictory, dialectical relationship of practice and theory that we can find ourselves and, if we lose ourselves sometimes, we will find ourselves again in the end.

Another concern I have regarding sectarian community-based programs is their extreme lack of humility, that makes them arrogant. It is for this reason that there is no space in the sectarian community-based program for dialogue, but only for polemics.

I am convinced that, not only in Brazil, but also in Latin America, it is impossible to cross the path of learning of democracy, how to make democracy, without confronting the community-based sectarianism and elitism as it represents the live expression of authoritarian traditions. And we are still in the process of learning how to make democracy. And the struggle for democracy must pass through the struggle against all types of authoritarianism.

I believe that one of our struggles, as progressive educators, is to learn to be less angry with respect to community-based sectarianism and elitism, but at the same time, be always alert to its possibility.

Carlos Torres: I would now like to turn to the question of language. Language constitutes identities. Both you and I know how difficult it is, for example, to say "I love you" or "I hate you" in a language different from our own. A greater problem is that the cultural capital of the socially subordinate classes, the poor, usually expresses itself in a language quite different from the middle-class language of the schools. This creates great problems for newcomers to a society who need to learn the dominant discourse or the national language of their new community. How should this issue of language be treated by educators?

Paulo Freire: The questions related to language have always concerned me and they never cease to be one of the preoccupations of my life. It was not an accident that at nineteen years of age, more or less, I began to teach Portuguese syntax with the same passion that I throw myself into pedagogical reflections or educational practice. I was always touched by language.

I am convinced that it is not possible to discuss language without discussing power, or without thinking about social classes and their contradictions. And, since I have mentioned social classes in the full process of radical changes, particularly in East Europe, I should make it clear that I do not feel, on the one hand, I am among those who until recently mystified Marx by making him God, and on the other hand, neither do I agree with those who now declare that Marx no longer has anything to say. Naturally a lot of things that Marx said will have to be rethought. Marx, in truth, was not God nor did he pretend to be God.

It is one thing to recognize the complexity of certain societies experiencing a highly advanced level of capitalism, which require a fine-tuning of Marxist tools of analysis so as to understand them better; it is another thing, because of the complexity referred to above, to negate the existence of social classes—the existence of contradictory interests among them. Another thing is to accept that class conflicts cannot, in themselves, explain everything, including the color of clouds on a particular Tuesday afternoon; it is yet another thing to definitively reject the existence of social classes. This is, however, the theme of our conversation. Let's return to the question of language.

The way that we are—the manner with which we eat, the possibility and even the very taste for eating, what to eat, the way we dress up, the way we behave in the world, how we find ourselves with others and the way we communicate, the level of education, our class position in the society to which we belong—all these things end up being part of our language, our thinking structure that, in turn, conditions us. It is for this very reason that traditional educators rigorously fail to teach us language. We experience ourselves in language, we socially create language, and finally we become linguistically competent.

For us progressive educators, it does not matter if we teach biology, the social sciences, or the national standard language, it is fundamental that we respect the cultural identity that passes through social classes of students. It is necessary to respect the students' language, its syntax, and its semantics. It is this respect that is not present when we disregard or minimally regard the discourse of children from subordinate classes. Particularly when we more than insinuate and make our dislike obvious for the way those children speak, the way they write, the way they think, by labeling their speech ugly, inferior, and incorrect. It is precisely this that also takes place in the so-called multicultural societies where the language and hegemonic culture smash and belittle the language and culture of the so-called minorities. Linguistic discrimination is a preconception of sex, race, and class as well. We have, in truth, to respect the so-called nonstandard language as much as we have to respect the background knowledge of the subordinate classes so that with this knowledge we can go beyond it.

Language represents one of the important aspects in the process of democratization of societies. Naturally, when we speak about the vernacular, we run the risk, on the one hand, of falling into elitism and consider the linguistic expression of lower classes as something ugly and inferior, and on the other hand, we run the risk of falling into community-based sectarianism and reject the importance and the very need that the subordinate classes have in mastering the dominant language. The need to master the dominant language is not only to survive but also the better to fight for the transformation of an unjust and cruel society where the subordinate groups are rejected, insulted, and humiliated.

Carlos Torres: We have discussed your past and present. Could you turn to consider your future? What do you have planned for the future, for after you leave your position as Secretary of Education?

Paulo Freire: This is, for me, an interesting question since today I am sixty-eight years old, almost sixty-nine, and I will be seventy next year. I feel, however, very young. Perhaps not so young when I have to take the stairs up to the fifth floor and not the elevator. My body, then, complains and reminds me that I am almost seventy years of age. I live, however, a full life because I love life.

Sometimes, now, I miss the conviviality of my books, my reading, and my writing. For this reason, I hope to return home. This is not the case because I feel a lack of support from Luiza Erundina, the extraordinary woman who is mayor, or because I lack the help of the able team with which I work. I miss my books and the almost ritualistic way in which I look at them, open them, and reread some pages that I had "visited" some time before. Sometimes, I stop here and there and I laugh at the markings I made in them, or at some innocent marks by my sons and daughters, who are now men and women. I remember then how I bequeathed to them my love for reading.

I was working on four different book projects when I was invited to be the Secretary of Education. These projects wait for me and I hope to take them on again.

What inheritance can I leave? Exactly one. I think that it could be said when I am no longer in this world: "Paulo Freire was a man who lived. He could not understand life and human existence without love and without the search for knowledge. Paulo Freire lived, loved, and attempted to know. For this very reason, he was a human being who was constantly curious."

It is this that I hope will be the expression of my passing through the world, even when all I have said and written about education may have submerged into silence.

Carlos Torres: Thank you.

EPILOGUE

Manifesto to Those Who,
by Leaving, Stay

All of us have experienced enormous satisfaction from developing, through our common effort, a new pedagogical project in the Municipal Secretary of Education. It does not matter that, because of our commitment, we have, from time to time, experienced anguish and suffering.

I am convinced that the Workers Party's proposals and principles to which Mayor Luiza Erundina gives life, are correct. These constitute the general principles of the governmental policies of which the educational policies that we have been implementing are a chapter.

I am not, rigorously, leaving the Municipal Secretary of Education or even leaving your company. Nor am I rejecting the old political and ideological options that preceded the creation of the Workers Party. In my youth I never imagined that the Workers Party would have developed, though I used to feel the need for its existence. I waited for more than forty years for the Workers Party to be created.

Even though I will no longer be the secretary, I will continue to be near you in one way or another. I will have more free time to take on another type of presence.

I am not leaving the fight, but simply moving to another front. The fight continues on the same. Wherever I am I will be as engaged as you are in favor of democratic, popular public schools.

People like, and have the right to like, different things. I like to write and to read. To write and read represent, as important moments, part of my struggle. I put this love of reading and writing at the service of a certain societal design whose realization, with a large number of colleagues, I, within the limits of my possibilities, have been working to create. The fundamental thing about this love I have been speaking about is to know in whose favor and for whom do I put it into practice.

My love for reading and writing is directed toward a certain utopia. This involves a certain course, a certain type of people. It is a love that has to do with the creation of a society that is less perverse, less discriminatory, less racist, less *machista* than the society that we now have. This love seeks to create a more open society, a society that serves the interests of the always unprotected and devalued subordinate classes, and not only the interests of the rich, the fortunate, the so-called "well-born."

For all this, to write not a mean, but lucid and courageous critique of the dominant classes will be one of my fronts of battle, as it has been for many of you.

I am loyal to the dream. My actions have been consonant with it. It has demanded ethics. I believe that ethics have to do with the coherence with which one lives in the world, the coherence between what one says and does. Hence, I do not fear criticism leveled against the work that was realized in this bureau in these two and a half years that I was here as secretary. I believe criticism, when leveled competently and ethically, makes our actions gain more depth and can lead to intelligent reorganization. We learn from our actions.

Continue to count on me in the construction of an educational politics, of a school with another "face," one that is more joyful, harmonious, and democratic.

POSTSCRIPT

São Paulo's
Education Revisited

by Ana Maria Saul

Introduction

It was a great pleasure to receive an invitation from Paulo Freire to write a postscript for this book. The invitation made me experience a double pleasure: On the one hand, I sensed a certain pride, a feeling of privilege, at being asked to write a chapter that would be included in the second edition of a book written by an internationally renowned author. On the other hand, I felt a great deal of satisfaction knowing I would write about a real experience that I had, for the most part, encountered as I worked with and learned from Paulo Freire. At the prospect of writing this postscript I experienced as well the actualization of the language of possibility in a context full of contingencies. It was here that Paulo Freire was able, despite extreme difficulties and great ideological differences, never to lose sight of his utopian dreams. Throughout the process Freire always served as a catalyst for the energies of a team charged with working to address the educational challenges in the city of São Paulo.

While I was at once filled with pleasure at the prospect of writing the postscript, I was overtaken at the same time by a sense of responsibility, since the "invitation-charge" from Paulo Freire solicited an up-to-date evaluation with commentaries measuring what had effectively taken place in the Department of Education during his tenure as secretary of education. The evaluation was to be made in reference to the various proposals Freire announced in interviews during the beginning of his administration and through the first months of his second year as the secretary of education in São Paulo. As Paulo Freire so clearly stated, the book, *Pedagogy of the City*, has an introductory character that points to what we had dreamed of accomplishing in the schools and to what is now being done to meet the goals we have established. Thus, I am presented with a great responsibility because, even though the book has an introductory character as highlighted by Paulo Freire, the proposals and discussions put forth in it are multifaceted. Thus to speak about their actualization and limitations requires an effort of selection and analysis that is, at the same time, balanced so as not to give the impression that one is avoiding self-congratulation or an exacerbated critique. For this reason, the proposal that I received to write this text presented itself contradictorily as a historical compromise that was both easy and difficult at the same time.

It was a historical compromise because I participated in Paulo Freire's administration—at his invitation—to coordinate the curricular restructuring for the Department of Education from the very beginning of his tenure. I have remained a part of the Department's educational team up to this forth year of Mayor Luiza Erundina de Souza's term in office. The ambiguity encountered in the task of writing this text springs directly from my personal involvement in the process of transforming the schools under the leadership of Freire. Thus this postscript is written with the subjectivity of someone who is immersed in the work, passionately involved in it, and who is coresponsible for the political and technical directorship of the schools. I have experienced great happiness and many disappointments while struggling with adversity during my years working on the curriculum. These experiences make the process of writing this evaluation complex. I am faced both with the ease and the difficulty of selecting and reporting on—in an analytical and critical form, within the limits of this text—the work accomplished.

Therefore, the reader should not expect a research report along the lines of those that must meet academic standards. This critical report is written by someone who has worked four years in this administration and who had reread many times the chapters written in this book. Nonetheless, this postscript describes the dreams that were realized and their limitations.

Searching for Criteria for the Selection of Critical Areas for Analysis

Certain criteria led me to select the areas of analysis about which I attempt to provide evaluative commentaries. One of them is the reoccurrence of certain issues and/or preoccupations that appear in the interviews with Paulo Freire in this book, which set the parameters of the leadership of the Department of Education in the city of São Paulo under the present government. The other is the meaning of certain occurrences that, although infrequent, undoubtedly capture the politics of the Department of Education in the city of São Paulo. I will begin the evaluation with the epilogue of the book where the "Manifesto" is synthesized in a manner of someone who, by leaving, stays.

What is mentioned in the epilogue does not constitute merely rhetoric in an emotional moment in which Paulo Freire was leaving the Department of Eduction, but an intention that became reality in two respects. The first is that Paulo Freire was able to put together a cohesive educational team around the political proposal of the Department of Education where he shared power with the team in which I had the privilege of participating. Freire was able to democratize the administration of the Department of Education through collective organizing that has permitted, even with his departure, the continuity of his proposals and principles that are still being discussed and exist in various phases of development. This is a rare fact in the Brazilian culture where the presence of administrators is so personalized and centralized that their absence, for whatever reasons, always causes serious ruptures in the proposals and in the working groups, leading to frequent alteration of direction that generates insecurities, lack of credibility in the administrations, and consequent destabilization in the work itself. Such has not been the case since Paulo Freire's departure from office. That this is the case is great testimony to his ability to democratize the administrative sector of the department.

In fact, both Paulo Freire and Luiza Erundina demonstrated extreme care in the administration of the city's schools. They searched, through frank dialogue, to solidify and ensure that the educational team would work with the secretary so as to provide continuity to the work developed during the two and a half years of Paulo Freire's administration.

The second aspect that becomes an explicit reality in the "Manifesto" was that Paulo Freire followed in his fight, as he had always done, the yearning for a democratic education by writing, giving lectures throughout Brazil and the world, and at the same time keeping abreast of the work being done by the city government and the city's Department of Education. Paulo Freire never avoided being present in discussions and analyses when asked. This characteristic is marked by its singularity, and therefore is highly significant.

The remaining issues to be discussed in the postscript were selectively based on the frequency in which they were raised in the interviews throughout the book and the degree to which they were relevant to the overall process of educational reform.

Throughout the interviews Freire singled out quantitative and qualitative deficits as great problems in Brazilian education. I will, therefore, highlight these two issues in order to evaluate the ways in which the deficits were addressed. I will call the reader's attention to the fact that the quality of education was not treated in any moment by this administration as a fetish but, on the contrary, whenever the issue of quality was raised, there was always clarity in terms of understanding of what it would mean to "change the face of the schools." This "changing of the face of the schools" was implicated in the continuous, persistent, and demanding work we were carrying out.

Confronting the Quantitative and Qualitative Deficits: A Critical Evaluation

In 1989, when Freire took office the effects of the neglect of the educational system by previous administrations were very visible, both in the deterioration of school buildings and also in the cultural morass, skepticism, and fear demonstrated by educators. Teacher preparation institutes as well were devalued at this time. Freire set about to invert priorities and turn the attention of his administration to the dispossessed.

Against the "chaos" we encountered, four priorities were established by the Department of Education directed by Paulo Freire, in dialogue with his colleagues:

1. Democratization and access.
2. Democratization of administration.
3. New quality of teaching.
4. Youth and adult education.

I will provide a synthesis of the achievements reached in each of these priority areas. In my evaluation I will follow the order in which the priorities are presented above. However, I should note that all of these priorities were tackled simultaneously. We could not wait for the resolution of the first in order to initiate the others. The reader will see some of the priority areas received more in-depth treatment from the beginning of implementation than did others.

In order to understand action taken in an effort to fulfill the first priority—Democratization of Access to School—it is necessary to present some data. Over ten million people live today in São Paulo and the city experiences an increase of three hundred thousand people each year. Given its urban status and the fact that it is considered the largest industrial complex in Latin America, São Paulo attracts a migrant population characterized by precarious life conditions in an exploited third-world country. These migrants look at São Paulo as a way to better their condition in life. In this important city that covers 1.509 square kilometers (approximately one square mile) the architecture displays areas with great buildings that can be compared with other cities around the world. At the same time, these towering buildings stand in sharp contrast to the surrounding shacks, shelters, and houses in dilapidated condition where the downtrodden and homeless representing the majority population in the streets live. In this city, today (1992) there are approximately one million unemployed people while seven million others live in shacks, shanty towns, and houses in deteriorating condition. The overall budget for the city in 1993 is $2,536,582,508.13.

Even though two million children and youths are enrolled in three school districts in elementary education in particular, approximately four-hundred-thousand children between the ages of seven through fourteen have not yet gone to school. To this alarming number one adds six-hundred-thousand preschool children who are locked out of classes due to lack of space, while 14 percent of youths and adults are illiterate. The sheer volume and gravity of these figures represent a great challenge to an administration whose goals are to redress the inequities of the subordinate classes by acknowledging that education is a necessary condition although not entirely sufficient for social transformation.

Today, after almost four years of the socialist administration, it is possible to provide the following picture concerning educational reform in São Paulo. One observes that the city, in view of the available economic resources, proposes to enroll approximately 30 percent of school-age children in basic education. By applying the 25 percent of the city's budget, as mandated by a city law in São Paulo, the city has today 771,730 students attending 688 schools in the public school system. This number represents only 42.10 percent of school age children who are enrolled in school.

The following is a breakdown of students attending school:

- 493,850 students in basic education, in 353 schools.
- 1,032 students, in five schools for deaf students
- 2,028 in a single professional school (high school level) where a teacher preparation course is also offered
- 194,976 children between 4 and 6 years of age, in 329 schools (kindergarten and preschool).

When compared with 1988, there is an increase of 120,358 students in the public school system—that is, an increase of 15.59 percent. This increase, on the one hand, is due to the expansion in the number of schools. Seventy-seven new schools were constructed, representing an increase of 11.19 percent in school space. There was also a great effort to maximize the use of existing school buildings by operating, generally, four different shifts of four hours each.

Night school, which occupies the same buildings as day school, serves almost eighty thousand students in the regular offerings as well as working students who follow a special curriculum designed as supplementary education.

We, however, consider that the increase in the construction of new schools still falls far short of our goals. This affirmation must be evaluated in two different contexts: On the one hand, there was the option to renovate 60 percent of the school buildings in the system, including general maintenance, remodeling and changes (really new construction) of buildings that were practically deteriorated. In terms of school furniture we initially bought 60,000 new desks for students. In addition, we purchased new sets of school equipment that represented the greatest acquisition and distribution of these articles to schools in the system in fifty-two years. These included: televisions, video casettes, sound machines, slide projectors, tape recorders, 825 microcomputers. We began regularly to provide the more commonly used materials to 40 percent of students, particularly in preschools, in order to provide relief to families who could ill afford to buy materials such as scissors, chalk, notebooks, pencils, etc. We deliberately invested in the purchase of seventy-eight thousand children's literature and other pedagogical books that filled the gap in reading rooms that were, for the most part, empty. The expansion of these materials represented an increase of 500 percent in relation to the period of 1986 to 1988.

The maintenance and construction of new schools became a priority in the first two years of Paulo Freire's administration in order to guarantee the effective functioning of the school system. The construction of new schools has slowed down considerably, due to cuts in federal grants to cities—particularly São Paulo because of political disagreements along party lines. In response, São Paulo has for the first time an administration that has implemented a school construction plan with monies coming only from its own budget. Today, there is still a great deal to do concerning the maintenance of schools. However, the rhythm has normalized to the extent that the most problematic cases have been addressed and solved.

I turn now to a discussion of the second priority: Democratization of administration. At no time in this political and educational administration did we think to democratize access to schools without first democratizing the administration itself, even though we were running the risk of losing to the cultural weight of authoritarianism embedded for almost five-hundred years in the history of our country.

In his role as administrator Paulo Freire always reminded us of the connection between the day-to-day routine of Brazilian schools and the society within which these schools are situated. He often called to our attention that the "oppressed

brings within him or her the oppressor," wishing to underline the necessary effort in the struggle for liberation so as
to achieve a more just and democratic society. The school
continues to reflect a class-based society and the resultant
class warfare, as well as imposed and institutionalized power.
It is necessary that we fight against the social injustices and
inequities, since for us to do so indicates movement toward
the betterment of the quality of education. It has not been
easy to fight for a democratic school administration; we continue to experience confrontation and conflict with conservative forces within and outside the administration that fear a
democratic transformation of the system.

The democratic administration constituted for us a question of honor that informed our actions from the very beginning of our administration. In the various interviews Paulo
Freire cited the devastating authoritarian context that characterized the preceding administration from 1986 to 1988.
Teachers were persecuted for going on strike; they were
subjected to ostracism and fired from their jobs. The more
progressive educational proposals were considered to be
communist-influenced and were thus blocked and ordered
out of schools, burned, or sold as used paper. The past
administration constituted a real reign of authoritarian terror
in the Sao Paulo public schools. The school constitution that
was approved the last day of the administration that preceded
Mayor Junio Quadros was suspended on the first day of his
administration.

One of the great values of the by-laws that were never
implemented—not even in the administration of Guiomar
Namo de Mello, nor in the mayoral tenure of Janio Quadros—was the proposal that schools have a deliberative
school council. In these past four years it has been possible
to have a school council because Paulo Freire, on his first day

as Secretary of Education, reestablished, with the Mayor's support, the Schools' Common Constitution within a perspective that respects educational professionals belonging to the city-wide school system. School councils became a reality under Paulo Freire's administration. Members were elected by the school community. During these past four years, there were four school council elections. These elections have not been without difficulties to the degree that conservative principals tried to manipulate the elections in an attempt to make the school councils more authoritarian, instead of allowing the councils a raison d'être to flourish where parents and community members engage in a real and democratic dialogue with school personnel about a wide range of educational issues not limited to their children's progress in school. There were instances in which the school councils made decisions that the administration and school personnel thought were wrong, to the extent that they impinged on human rights. In such situations, the administrators and school personnel met with the school council to discuss their deliberations. These discussions always followed a pedagogical perspective taking into consideration that the work with the school council is educationally necessary.

The work with the school councils was not always well understood even by the school community that felt school issues traditionally belong only to teachers and specialists. Teachers and school specialists often expected to be delegated the power to decide on what to teach as well as deal with issues of control and discipline. Some teachers even thought it appropriate to apply physical and moral punishment, if they deemed it necessary.

Democratic administration is not only necessary in schools, but also in the government to counter the passivity toward hierarchical power and toward the delegated power that each time reinforces a society's authoritarianism that never contributes positively toward a democratic society.

During the two and a half years of Freire's administration, we simultaneously experienced the tensions of power between the principal and school specialists' authority and the democratization and sharing of power with teachers, students, and parents. We discussed with schools and unions the by-laws of the school constitution and the necessary changes to the school constitution in the beginning of Freire's administration. It would have been absolutely antidemocratic to have presented to the city council and the school council a ready-made set of proposed by-laws without the input of parents, teachers, students, and community members. We could not and should have not run the risk of committing the "sin of power" obtained through elections only to use this power arbitrarily. For this reason, during the first three years of the administration we met with schools, unions, parents, different sectors of government, and the legislative body to develop proposals that would be voted on as the guiding by-laws of the Common Constitution of Schools.

It is only now, in the fourth year of the administration, that these negotiations have been finalized. The Bureau of Education backed off from various aspects of the Constitution, not without a fight, but always respecting the rules of the democratic game. We lost, for example, the opportunity to have elections of school principals. The election of principals constituted a major hope of Freire's administration, but this proposal was defeated overwhelmingly by the majority of schools.

However, we won, for example, the right to have a deliberative school council with more power than before with equal representation of teachers, parents, staff, educational specialists, and community members. This council is responsible for the elaboration and the evaluation of the school plan. The school councils have representatives from the ten regions that divide the city of Sao Paulo, and they organize themselves in regional chapters of school councils. These regional councils are involved not only in school-related issues, but are also part of the city budget planning.

The adopted school by-laws achieved goals of historical significance, such as the possibility that teachers' full-time load include work time with students, work time for collective planning, time for ongoing professional development, time to work with the community, and time for student evaluation.

After over one-hundred meetings and negotiations the school by-laws were approved unanimously by the city council and signed by the mayor in a public ceremony on June 26, 1992, attended by school representatives, the legislature, school union representatives, and school personnel and officials. The passage of the school by-laws represented for us a great democratic victory.

The present School Constitution that was also developed through meetings and negotiations presents no fewer difficulties. The basic tenets of the present School Constitution are the democratization of both the school administration and the curriculum. With respect to the curiculum the following was proposed: a school structure divided into three parts; autonomy in the development of school proposals; and a system of rigorous but democratic teacher evaluation that will neutralize the threatening power inherent in conventional evaluation mechanisms. A continous evaluation was proposed that would emphasize both process and product. These evaluations will be returned to both students and parents with an interpretive goal of research and enhancement of the school plan.

Work with the school councils and the regional and council chapters is being strengthened. In the process we have witnessed both success and drawbacks. The movement is slower than what one would like to see. The participation and community organization that represent the backbone of the school council concept by including the community as an equal partner in the construction of the quality public education continues to be somewhat weak. Given the sociohistorical conditions of the Brazilian reality, this is to be expected.

We could cite some actions that support our democratic administration: Parent participation and ongoing training meetings with school guards and cafeteria workers represent part of Freire's dream that has been now realized. The first meeting took place timidly after a conversation with Paulo Freire who believed that it was the appropriate moment to begin such initiatives. After discussion with some advisors, Freire asked us to put the proposal on paper. We complied and returned to discuss the proposal with him. The project was presented and amply discussed in one of the schools. It was decided that it would be implemented first in a region of the city that showed interest in doing so. The proposal was considered to be of great worth. Three coordinators from the Education Action Nucleus volunteered and the work began in one of the regions in the East Zone of the city. Today, various Education Action Nuclei develop projects, recreating existing ones, by themselves and with parents.

We have approximately forty groups participating in parent training. Many of these groups are coordinated by parents themselves. Work with parents, via the school councils and training groups, culminated in two-parent conferences developed and coordinated by parents with the total support of the Bureau of Education. The first conference took place in December 1991, and the second was organized in July 1992. Parent organizations represented the real and effective support both in discussions concerning the school system's by-laws and in the Bureau of Education discussions with respect to budget priorities alongside the city councils for approval of legal projects.

The work with the community was crystallized with a project called "in favor of life, not violence." This project came to life due to certain problems in the school environment, including bloodshed and other depredation. The work carried out with the community has yielded some very positive results in the scholastic community, by creating public spheres where the community can discuss and debate problems in an effort to resolve them. Some of the steps that have been taken include the utilization by the community of school equipment during weekends, principally when the community begins to valorize schools by understanding what schools do and can do, especially when the community is asked to participate in schools.

There is still a great deal to do in the journey to democratize schools and organize the community. One of the statutes developed during this administration that was amply discussed and now awaits, at this very moment, the legislature's approval, is the creation of an Education City Council. This organization would bring together ample participation of different sectors representative of the population at large. This democratically constituted council would have a fundamental role in decisions regarding citywide education.

Another action initiated by Freire's administration that has had a great impact throughout the city of São Paulo is Project AIDS. This project was initiated with the cooperation of the Bureau of Health, with the goal of addressing the schools' requests for information and AIDS-prevention strategies. Various workshops to deal with AIDS issues, including society's discrimination against HIV virus carriers, have been held. Today, the generation of children born with the AIDS virus are beginning to come to school and the mayor of São Paulo has opened the schools' doors wide so as to welcome these children. Opening school doors to HIV-infected children did not occur without trauma and rejection. However, due to the effective education given by Project AIDS, the Bureau of Education has received numerous positive newspaper and television reports that acknowledge the importance of Project AIDS in minimizing the hardships of students who are HIV virus carriers. The group that coordinates Project AIDS in the Bureau of Education has trained one thousand individuals who are now part of the project. In addition to their professional responsibilities in schools, these trained individuals work four hours weekly for specific Project AIDS tasks for which they are renumerated.

New Quality of Education

The new quality of education progressed, as announced by Paulo Freire in the various interviews included in this book, with two objectives: the reorientation of the curriculum and ongoing teacher education.

The reorientation of the curriculum was proposed from the very beginning of Freire's administration as a movement that opposed the so-called educational packets that are generally imposed on schools. The reorientation was characterized by the development of a process curriculum within a perspective of liberating education. In order to carry this out, it was necessary to work out a process that called for greater participation of the school community concerning the direction and action of the curriculum—understood generally as the very pedagogical proposal of the school, while respecting and motivating school autonomy.

The reorientation of the curriculum presented as a process of collective development was situated in the valoration of the unity of theory and practice and understood as a constant dialogue among different specialists from different areas of knowledge, which required a great effort of understanding, preparation, and even creation. This requires comprehension in the sense of the radical transformation of "making curriculum," "thinking," and "living" the curriculum in a manner very different from the conventional way of viewing curriculum in our culture. This latter view may be identified as the paradigmatic technical-linear. The ongoing teacher education that was proposed by Freire's administration represents the foundation supporting the process of reorientation of the curriculum. The ongoing teacher education process has required great creativity in its elaboration and execution, given the great number of teachers involved (35,131).

The two first stages of this movement, problematization and systematization (on its first level), have been implemented systemwide in all degrees and patterns of teaching. The Bureau of Education supports these projects, either by providing materials or by paying teachers involved in the teacher education project to attend classes.

Another established work objective in the Reorientation of Curriculum Movement is the art of teaching via an interdisciplinary focus—a focus that takes generative themes as a point of departure. It begins with the preliminary study of the local reality, identifying the geographic conditions, tools, human, and work relations, as well as values and social injustice. The analysis of this information leads to the identification of significant contexts from which the generative themes are developed. For example:

- Work and leisure: road to security.
- It is possible to live without violence.
- School and the interaction of humans in the occupation of space.
- Work and life: How does one construct this relationship?
- Citizenship: How to achieve it and how to keep it.
- Community: Conviviality, conscienciousness, and transformation.
- Neighborhood.
- Access, occupation, and appropriation of space by humans.

From these themes, content in different areas of human knowledge is selected and developed so that students can understand the themes, generate new themes, organize and/or produce knowledge that enables them critically to interpret the reality within which they live while expanding their reading of the world. Up to now, more than 200 from a list of 353 elementary schools have adhered to an interdisciplinary focus via the creative-theme.

The multidisciplinary teams from the Education Action Nucleus of the Department of Technical Orientation and the pilot schools (ten elementary that joined the projects) with mentoring from university professors, are working keenly in the collective development of the proposal of interdisciplinary focus, elaborating its description, establishing its foundation, its basic procedures, and its results.

This proposal is now in the expansion phase, with the addition of new elementary schools. These schools have as reference the initial work done by the ten pilot schools, and the guidance given by the Education Action Nucleus. These schools also receive assistance from the multidisciplinary teams and their respective Education Action Nucleus from the Department of Technical Orientation. They also receive support from the University of São Paulo, the Ponticifica Catholic University, and the University of Campinas. The interdisciplinary focus is also the goal that informs the development of curricular proposals for Early Childhood Education and Adult Education.

The program of teacher education has the following basic goals:

- The conceptualization of the desired school that has as its major goal the development of a new pedagogy;
- The need to supply elements of basic education to teachers, in different areas of human knowledge;
- The appropriation by educators of new scientific/technological advances of human knowledge that can contribute toward the enhancement of the quality of the desired school.

There are multiple variations in the ongoing teacher education program. Nevertheless, the basic proposal of teacher education should guarantee the principle of action/reflection/action; that is to say, the educators use their own practice as a point of departure for discussion, they express their theoretical underpinnings with depth, and they advance their foundations reconstructing their practice within the perspective of transformative education.

The central work of teacher education is implemented by the teacher-education teams. This work has already been described regarding its foundations and results.

The teacher education group offers to the educators the opportunity for exchange in which the social, affective, and cognitive being is valorized. In this manner, one safeguards the personal and professional identity of the educator while, at the same time, one gives educators the opportunity to find themselves in the group or outside of it. The themes that emerge are studied within the perspective of the collective construction of knowledge. In this process, one searches for an understanding of the heterogeneous, its confrontation, and the possibility of rupturing crystallized postures.

Ongoing teacher education has been developed through a new partnership with the university, with the understanding that both the teachers from the city schools and the university professors have a great deal to learn from each other. The group for parent training was constituted in another important relationship to integrate the school with the community. The parents meet periodically with the teachers so they can discuss issues relative to the education of their children. These encounters make it possible for parents to organize and bring to school problems to be resolved in their own communities.

The actions of the reorientation of the curriculum and ongoing teacher education program along with other actions of the Bureau of Education are, without a doubt, factors that determined the lower level of student failure these past four years. Without these advances in our educational procedure, there would have been approximately 45,155 students kept back in grade, enlarging the statistics of those who are temporarily excluded from a completed education. The failure of students diminished considerably in all the elementary grades, principally in first and fifth grades, where, traditionally, the rate of failure is greater.

The level of failure in Sãn Paulo was reduced to 22 percent while the average rate of failure in Brazil has reached 50 percent. With respect to school dropouts, the rate in 1992 remained at 5 percent in São Paulo, making our student dropout rate one of the lowest in the world. These figures alone speak volumes in support of a true democratization of education.

Acknowledgments

Many of the translated chapters were prepared with Alexandre Oliveira, who is gratefully acknowledged.

PART ONE

Chapter 1: Interview given to *Leia*.

Chapter 2: Interview given to the journal *Escola Nova*, São Paulo, Brazil, February 26, 1989.

Chapter 3: Interview given to the journal *Psicologia*, of the São Paulo Board of Psychology, in March 1989. Translated with Alexandre Oliveira.

Chapter 4: Interview given to the Education Workers' Union of Minas Gerais, in March 1989. Translated with Alexandre Oliveira.

Chapter 5: Interview given to the Italian journal *Terra Nuova* on May 6, 1989. Translated with Alexandre Oliveira.

Chapter 6: Interview given on August 9, 1989, to *Convergence* magazine (International Council for Adult Education, Canada). Translated with Alexandre Oliveira.

167